MONSTER!

MONSTER!

True Tales from a Show Biz Life

ERIC HALL

BⱮXTREE

First published in 1998 by Boxtree, an imprint of Macmillan Publishers Ltd,
25 Eccleston Place, London, SW1W 9NF and Basingstoke

Associated companies throughout the world

ISBN 0 7522 2408 5

9 8 7 6 5 4 3 2 1

A CIP catalogue record for this book is available from the British Library

Typeset by Blackjacks

Printed by Mackays of Chatham PLC, Chatham, Kent

Photographs: family – Eric Hall; Bolan, Mercury, Richards – Peter Vernon;
Britt Ekland – Doug McKenzie; Barbara Windsor – *Sunday Mirror*;
Beadle, Sherwood, Venables, Eva, Brady, Wise – *Sunday People*.

This book is dedicated to my late dad, Benny, who I miss terribly even now, my brother Terry and my nephew Eamon who were both taken from this life far too soon, and my grandparents Sarah and Sam Hiller and Katie Hall.

Chapter One

I've worked with some of the greatest showbiz and sporting stars in the world and whenever I'm with one of them I say to myself: 'I wonder what my grandmother is thinking if she's looking down on me now.'

I hope she'd be proud of the little Jewish lad from London's East End. She was Sarah Hiller, the mother of my lovely mum Eva, and I loved her to death. Even as a teenager I preferred to visit my grandparents, Sarah and Sam, and listen to their wonderful Jewish stories than go to the cinema or dances with the other lads.

But, I've more than made up for it since by meeting most of the stars they were watching on the silver screen and, as for dancing, I've even partnered that glorious lady Ginger Rogers. I may not have had as much elegance as Fred Astaire but it would still have come as a monster shock to the boys from Bethnal Green.

I was born in Old Nicholl Street in Shoreditch, which is within the sound of Bow Bells so I am an official cockney. My date of birth is 1 November 19 something-ish. The actual year of my birth is known only to my family and closest friends. I keep it a secret from everyone else because of a tip I was given by the late, great George Burns who I met in Hollywood when he was still relatively young – only in his late seventies.

When I asked George how old he actually was he replied: 'You know that most women lie about their age by knocking off a few years when asked how old they are, well I do the opposite. I add years on because when I tell people I'm such-and-such and they say "Really George, you look sensational" it actually does make me feel younger than I am.' It's advice I've followed ever since and I can tell you it works because my ego is given a monster boost every 1 November when I lie about my age.

It was on one of my birthdays, when I was eight or nine, that I discovered for the first time that I had a head for business. My family had moved up the road from Shoreditch to Bethnal Green and there was a lad living on our estate who was a boring little schmuck but who also happened to be totally brilliant at everything he did. I don't remember his full name, I think it was Dennis something or other, and he was the school swat.

He always did his homework and finished top of the class in all the exams. He was always well behaved, tidy and, more importantly, when Bonfire Night came around he made the best Guy Fawkes anyone had ever seen. It was a masterpiece with more lights than the Blackpool Illuminations and not even the meanest person, and there were not too many of those in the East End in those days, could resist dipping their hands into their pockets when asked if they could spare a penny for this particular Guy.

Not being daft, Dennis chose Bethnal Green underground station as his pitch – a very busy spot with thousands of passengers passing through in the rush hours. But although he was clever he wasn't street-wise and there was one major problem for the boy genius. The station had four entrances and exits and, naturally, he could only cover one of them.

That's where my brothers Benny and Allen and I stepped in. We waited to see which entrance Dennis chose, then I would go to one of the others while Benny took the third and Allen the fourth. When the punters came by we'd shout 'Penny for the Guy, mister' and when they asked where it was we just pointed to where Dennis was standing with his wonderful creation and, bingo, they paid up.

He never did discover our scam and that was not the only one we pulled on the schmuck. We also got our Christmas money courtesy of Dennis because he was the kid who delivered the newspapers in the area – well, he would, wouldn't he?

Dennis obviously expected his customers to be generous with their tips when Christmas came around but Benny and I figured none of them really knew who their paper boy was. After all, he had to get up at the crack of dawn to deliver the papers and they were still in bed. So, two weeks-ish before Christmas, Benny and I would divide up the houses on the round and start knocking on all the doors saying 'Paper boy, Merry Christmas'.

Again, like good East Enders, they never refused to put their hands in their pockets and the cash went into ours. Dennis never could figure out why, when he started knocking on doors a week or so later to say he was the paper boy they all told him to get lost.

I suppose some people would describe the strokes we pulled on poor little Dennis as cheating, but we preferred to use that lovely Jewish word 'chutzpah' which basically means having the cheek of the devil but good luck to you if you can get away with it. Anyhow, it was my first business venture and I got a buzz out of it so I wasn't all that bothered about what Dennis thought.

By the time I was in my early teens I was into what Arthur Daly would call another nice little earner. This one came courtesy of another branch of the family, known as The Mintzes. There were three brothers, named Bert, Izzy and Maurice, who was automatically known as Morrie. Can you imagine having a name like Morrie Mintz at a time when one of the most famous adverts on the television was for 'Murray Mints, the too good to hurry mints'.

Naturally Morrie was soon nicknamed 'Too Good' and for me his family turned out to be 'Very Good' because Izzy's business was selling rosettes at all the big sporting venues in London and he invited me to help him. 'Want to make a few quid at the weekends?' he asked. Was he sure? I'd have worked all week for a few quid in those days, but as it turned out, I was set to make even more money out of the deal than I'd ever dreamed of before then.

I discovered Izzy had always fallen in line with all the other sellers by waiting at the football stadium until the coaches arrived from Birmingham, Manchester, Liverpool or wherever, then trying to out-run everyone to get to them first with the rosettes.

As he was prepared to pay me half of what they sold for, which was about two and six in old money, I realized I was on to a small fortune on a good day. But even at that age I was smart enough to come up with a plan that I knew would guarantee that I made even more money.

Izzy wasn't too happy when I first told him I had an idea that would increase profits for just a little more effort and outlay. 'You are thirteen years old, only been in the business five minutes yet already you think you can run it better than me,' he yelled. But he soon changed his tune when I'd finished talking. My plan was to steal a march on all our rivals by reaching the fans before they started their journey. In other words, selling to them when they got on the coaches, not when they got off in London. I also suggested we could have someone at the motorway service stations grabbing the punters when they stopped for a tea break. Izzy loved the idea but the competitors were livid when they discovered fans arriving at Wembley or Highbury with rosettes already pinned to their jackets.

It wasn't long before they worked out who it was that was beating them to the punch because Izzy's rosettes were made by his sister Millie and were very distinctive. Soon they were all making the trip north on the Friday night before a big match.

But, by the time they'd caught up, my earnings had increased by about 200 percent and, by schoolboy standards, I was a millionaire.

I also made a killing whenever there was an international at Wembley involving a foreign team.

We put the prices up to five bob for those matches anyhow but often when the Germans, French or Italians asked me how much a rosette was I'd just put up five fingers. And it was amazing how many of them were confused and took out a £5 note thinking that's what I meant. Of course, I wasn't going to tell they were mistaken, was I?

I certainly made more from those early business exploits than from the theatrical exploits my mum Eva had planned for me. My marvellous father Benny was a London cabby but I don't think he ever found out how much of his hard-earned money went into sending me to the Italia Conte drama school. I went to hundreds of auditions, mainly for musicals. My party piece was singing the Judy Garland hit 'Over The Rainbow', but I was never offered a part until one day the lady from the agency rang my mum and said excitedly, 'Mrs Hall, your boy Eric has been accepted for a spot in the new Lionel Bart musical *Oliver*.'

When my mum told me about it I got in all of a dither and told her I couldn't possible accept the part. 'Why ever not, bubbelah?' she asked. 'Because I don't do parts, I only do auditions,' I told her.

But, in fact, I did take the role which was as one of the urchins in that great number 'You've Got To Pick A Pocket Or Two'. It was quite appropriate, I suppose, considering how I'd picked the pockets of Dennis and the football punters over the years.

It turned out to be the only job I ever had in the theatre – obviously my reviews were not good enough – but as I soon discovered, I was destined to be on the other side of the curtain, as it were, in the world of showbiz.

Incidentally, for those non-Jewish readers, let me explain that word 'bubbelah'. It's a Yiddish word used to describe someone you love and my mum never called me anything else. 'Don't worry bubbelah, you'll be fine,' my mum told me when I was five years old and on my way to my first day at school. 'There will be lots of other little boys and girls to play with, bubbelah. And, don't forget, bubbelah, I'll be outside waiting for you when school is over. And make sure you eat all your dinner, bubbelah.' It was bubbelah this and bubbelah that all the way to the door. Sure enough she was waiting when I came out – actually I don't think she went home – and immediately asked: 'So what did you learn on your first day in school, bubbelah?' 'I discovered that my name is Eric,' I told her.

Anyhow, she finally accepted that I wasn't going to be the next Laurence Olivier and I had to find a job when I left school. My uncle, Tony Hiller the great songwriter, about whom more later, said he could fix me up at a firm called Mills Music Publishers in Denmark Street, London's Tin Pan Alley at that time. 'You'll only be in the packing department and making the tea and all that stuff, but it's a start,' he told me.

It sounded great and I was only too happy to go to work in a place where I knew I would be able to see a lot of famous faces every day. When I arrived I was introduced to another young lad starting in his first job. He was going to be a fellow packer and his name was Reg Dwight.

Little did I know on that first day in Denmark Street that I was meeting one of the most famous of all the people I was to be associated with in my life. Reg Dwight, who at that time had only one claim to fame – his uncle Roy had played in the FA Cup for Nottingham Forest in 1959 – was soon to change his name to Elton John, and I was to become the managing director of his first record company, Rocket Records, and the publishing arm of the business, Big Pig Music.

In those day, however, he was just another cocky kid like myself with long hair (it's true I swear) and glasses, who used to wear those dungaree-type things and brightly coloured shirts that were popular in the 1960s.

If I'd had to take a guess then what young Reg would do in the future I'd have said he'd be an impersonator because he was always taking off all the top stars of the day, including the women. But, as I was to discover, when Reg became Elton he'd didn't need to copy anyone to become a star. He was unique and soon people would be trying to impersonate him.

Chapter Two

When my uncle Tony told me I'd be starting at the bottom in Mills Music he wasn't joking. Reg and I had to go out and buy the bacon sandwiches and cups of tea at Julie's Cafe in Denmark Street and generally be everyone's 'gofer' as well as run the packing department. But it was still monster, monster exciting for us to see all the top singers and songwriters of the time and to feel we were now part of the big showbiz world that was then centred on London.

There was also an early meeting for me with some of the football stars who I would later work with as an agent. Terry Venables was a very good singer and was once a member of the Joe Loss Orchestra (not many people know that, as Michael Caine might say) and I remember him coming to our office one day in 1965, along with George Graham and other members of the Chelsea team. A number of Chelsea players, including George and Terry, had recently been disciplined by their manager for breaking a curfew and the media had followed them to our office. The players hid in the packing department and pretended to work there.

I bet Terry never imagined when he and George did the jobs of Reg Dwight and Eric Hall that one day Reg would be a superstar and I'd be Terry's agent. Other top names like Adam Faith were also regular visitors to our firm but it was a bunch of lads who, like Reg and myself, were working in various Tin Pan Alley firms at the time who were to become the real icons of the pop scene.

One of the members of the Denmark Street gang was a skinny kid named David Jones. He changed his name to Dave Bowie some years later. Another gang member was Steve Marriott, the first lead singer of The Small Faces. It was such an exciting time in the music industry I suppose it's not surprising that we all felt anything was possible, although reaching the heights that Reg Dwight and David Jones eventually did would have been pushing even our dreams to their outer limits.

My days at Mills Music came to an end because they claimed I was a bad packer. The man in charge of the company, Cyril Gee, wore a bowler hat to work every day and on one occasion he walked into the packing department and, placing his hat on top of a pile of the old-fashioned 78 records, said 'Send that lot off to our office in America.'

Naturally I thought he wanted me to send the bowler hat as well as the records and, even though I thought it was a strange thing to do, who was I to argue with the boss? So I packed up the hat and the records and sent the parcel. An hour or so later his secretary, Jo Wright, who later changed her name and became Jo Gurnett, the agent for stars like Terry Wogan, Kenny Everett and Gloria Hunniford, phoned and asked if Mr Gee had left his hat in the packing department. It was only then that I realized I'd made a ricket but instead of owning up I denied all knowledge of it – which was not a very clever move as I was soon to discover. I'd overlooked the fact that I was a useless packer and by the time the parcel had reached Soho Square sorting office it was in tatters – all the records were broken and the hat was looking very much the worse for wear. The parcel was sent back to Mills Music and I was fingered as the culprit who had packed it.

Soon after that I was told my services were no longer required and it was explained to me that Mr Gee had not seen the funny side of the story. But my own version of the real reason for my departure is slightly different. Reg was already enjoying camping it up a bit and, as it happened, the head of our department – a man named Freddie Hartnell – was definitely camp. I was told later that Cyril Gee had decided we no longer needed two lads in the packing department and had ordered Freddie to let one of us go. I don't think it would need a genius to work out that it was the rebellious and very un-camp Eric Hall who would be looking for a new job. But I never told Elton that – until now – and I certainly didn't hold any grudges against him because the gang stayed together even though I'd moved down the road to a company called Lawrence Wright Music.

Lawrence Wright was a very famous songwriter who worked under the name of Horatio Nicholls. He had written hundreds of pre-pop era hits including 'Among My Souvenirs' and 'Hang Out The Washing On The Siegfried Line'. By now he was well into his eighties and could only get about in a wheelchair but he came to work every day and was still writing songs. We were the only publishing house in the street with a piano in the reception area as Lawrence was unable to get up the stairs. He would sit at that piano to write his songs and was usually gone by lunchtime.

The lads in the gang would come to my office in their lunch break and start tinkering on the piano. My immediate boss then was a man named Mr Mack who was obviously in the wrong business because if he ever caught us playing the piano he'd yell at me: 'Hall, get your mates off that piano, they're driving me mad with their so-called music.' If only he knew how many records Elton John, David Bowie and Steve Marriott would sell between them and how much money they'd make with that 'so-called music'.

When we weren't playing the piano the gang spent the lunch hour at one of three venues in the area, depending on the state of our finances. If we were flush it was the Tin Pan Alley Club where we could mix with all the stars. As the funds got lower it was Giaconda, an Italian restaurant where we drank cappuccino and ate spaghetti. And when we were skint at the end of the month it was Julie's Cafe for a cup of tea and a cheese roll.

Talking of finances, when I first started work at Mills Music I had to go a whole month without any wages and when I did get paid it was by cheque. 'What am I supposed to do with this?' I asked, to be told I'd have to open a bank account. So I did, in Barclays Bank in Soho Square and I've still got my account there to this day.

One of the colourful characters I met at The Tin Pan Alley Club was a lovely old boy named Harry Leon who, like Lawrence Wright, had written a whole string of hit songs under a pseudonym which, in his case, was Noel, and came from spelling Leon backwards. He wrote classics like 'Sally' and 'What More Can I Say' but, unfortunately, had no business sense and often sold the rights of his songs to anyone who'd pay him a fiver so he could buy a bottle of port. That was all he got for selling the rights of 'Sally' to the lady who made it famous, Gracie Fields.

He got the credit on the records and song sheets but it was Gracie who picked up all the cash. So, it was no surprise that by the time we met, Harry was down on his luck. He'd come into my office and say 'Young Eric, can you lend me half a crown to buy a glass of port?' If it was the time of the month when I had money I couldn't refuse, even though I knew I'd never get it back. But I'd get my money's worth by asking him to sit at the piano and play a few of his hits. And Mr Mack, the man who threw out the pop stars of the future, had no objection to this brand of music.

He'd come and join us over some of the great old songs and soon all three of us would be crying like babies. They cried because of the memories it brought back for them and I cried because I wasn't getting back my half a crown.

It was occasions like that which prepared me for the day when I would move out on my own as a record promoter with some of the music industry's biggest companies and work with a host of enter-tainment greats on both sides of the Atlantic in the next two decades.

Chapter Three

my first job as a record promoter was for a man named Phil Solomons who owned a record company called Major Minor but was better known in the 1960s as the man who started Radio Caroline. Radio Caroline was the station based on a ship off the Kent coast which, like Radio Luxembourg, challenged the BBC monopoly and led eventually to all the music stations we have now.

I was thrilled to be involved in the record-plugging business but I almost got the sack for something which had nothing to do with pop music. Solomons' wife, Dorothy, was a theatrical agent whose clients included The Bachelors, Frank Carson, Lena Zavaroni, Freddy 'Parrot Face' Davies and many, many more. As Hughie Green was on her books it was probably no coincidence that she also finished up with all the winners of his *Opportunity Knocks* series as her clients. My problem started because Phil and Dorothy shared the same office in Great Marlborough Street and I often used to help out in her business if I wasn't too busy.

Soon after I started work for the Solomons there was a summer show at Blackpool which featured many of Dorothy's clients. It was called *The Opportunity Knocks Winners' Show* and one of the spin-offs was a programme giving background details of all the winning acts. 'Dorothy is producing the programme so see if you can give her a hand by getting some sponsors to buy a page in it,' Phil told me.

I tried Thames Television and a few other companies without any luck. Then I had the bright idea of calling Hughie Green – after all I figured he had made a pile of money out of the show so he could afford to pay for a page. I found Hughie's private number and rang to ask if he wanted to buy a page. 'It need just say congratulations to all the winners from Hughie Green,' I told him. It was then that I discovered that perhaps it wasn't such a bright idea after all.

I have never heard language like it before or since. The air was blue as Hughie told me exactly what he thought of my request and of the cheeky young pup who'd made it. He was so incensed he contacted Phil Solomons and told him to sack me on the spot. Luckily for me, Phil realized it was nothing to do with my real job and calmed Hughie by telling him I'd been a bit naive but at least I'd been conscientious.

Oddly enough I next met Hughie Green over thirty years later, just before he died. I was in the Wellington Hospital for a hernia opera-tion – in fact it was a bilateral which the surgeon, Mr Geoffrey Glazer, explained was a double hernia. I couldn't help saying 'Trust me to get a double, Glazer.' We got on famously after that and one day he asked if I knew Hughie Green. I said our paths had once crossed but didn't elaborate and the doctor then told me that Hughie was also one of his patients and was 'not at all well'.

Just down the road from the Wellington is the Jewish restaurant Harry Morgan's, and on my next visit who should I see in there but Hughie Green. I couldn't help introducing myself. 'My name is Eric Hall, do you remember me?' I asked. 'Yes, you are the football agent,' said Hughie. I then reminded him of the incident with Phil Solomons all those years earlier. He had a good laugh about it and said he was glad I hadn't got the sack. It was soon after our meeting that he died and I was delighted I'd had the chance to clear the air about our little misunderstanding.

But I digress. With Major Minor I proved that I was one of the best pluggers in the business by getting our records promoted on Radio One.

As everyone knew at the time, the Beeb hated Radio Caroline and no-one could figure how I was managing to persuade Radio One to give plays to stars like Karen Young, Malcolm Roberts, Mikki and Griff, David McWilliams and many more who were contracted to Major Minor who in turn owned Radio Caroline. The reason was simple. I worked harder than the others and we had good records which Radio One just couldn't ignore. I had my first number one hit for Major Minor with a record called 'Mony Mony' by Tommy James and the Chantells. Radio Caroline was obviously pushing it but the record couldn't have made it to the top without lots of air-time on Radio One and Phil Solomons knew it.

I only ever went to Radio Caroline once: when I accompanied Jimmy Hoolihan, who was Phil's right-hand man. Jimmy used to make a weekly delivery of the latest records and the wages for the DJs and I'll always remember the day of my visit because the late, great Kenny Everett was on duty. As we were about to leave Kenny leant over the side of the ship and yelled at Jimmy, 'The wages are short again, I've had enough of this.' 'Take it up with Mr Solomons, it's not my fault,' said Jimmy. But Kenny was so angry he tried to grab Jimmy and fell into the sea. I monster swear it's true and that Kenny's career could have come to an abrupt and early end right then if someone hadn't been smart with the lifebelt.

That early contact with people like Kenny, Emperor Roscoe, David Hamilton, David Jensen and all the other Caroline and Luxembourg disc jockeys was to be of great help to me later in my record-promoting days when they had left the 'pirate' ranks and become establishment names.

When I decided to leave Phil Solomons in order to broaden my horizons even further I returned to the music publishing side of the business. I joined a company called Cyril Shane Publishing where I was responsible for taking a song from its birth with the writer, placing it with the right artist and then making and promoting the record. It was a very satisfying feeling to know that having started in the trade with Mills Music Publishers as a menial packer I was now back in the same game only a few years later as the main man. Whereas Mr Mack used to tell me to 'get your mates out' when I was with Lawrence Wright in Denmark Street I was now the guvnor telling other lads to clear off from our offices in Baker Street.

Among the artists I worked with at Cyril's were The Hollies and Herman's Hermits who were linked to the company because the wonderful Jack Fishman wrote most of their hits. He was an old Jewish gent who had been in a concentration camp during the war but had survived and now produced the most wonderful lyrics. The Hollies' 'He Aint Heavy He's My Brother' was one of the biggest hits we had during my stay with Cyril Shane Publishing and I still remember Jack sitting down and writing those lyrics. He'd heard the song performed in either Italian or French, I can't remember which, and had liked the tune so much we bought the rights to it and then Jack went into action. He didn't just translate the original lyric but wrote a whole new set of words.

I've always loved songwriters, probably because of the affection I have for my uncle, the songwriter Tony Hiller who wrote many hits including 'Save Your Kisses For Me'. Although I once tried my hand at songwriting I unfortunately had not inherited his talent. I kept getting close without ever quite making it. My efforts included 'Tea For One', 'I Could Have Danced All Day', 'Don't Go Breaking My Legs' and many, many more.

There is a tradition that when songwriters die their biggest hit is played at their funeral. I remember going to the funeral of the legendary Jimmy Kennedy and they played his great number 'South Of The Border'. I was with Bill Martin, another great songwriter, who said as we left the funeral that he hoped that they would do that for him when he passed on. 'In that case you are going to have to write a monster new hit before you go,' I said. 'Why is that?' he asked. 'Because we'll all look stupid standing at your graveside singing "Congratulations",' I told him. That was the song that had almost won the Eurovision Song Contest for Cliff Richard and was one of Bill's biggest hits – so far!

Many people may not know that writers and publishers of songs make most of their money from the Performing Rights fees which are payable every time a song is played on the TV or radio. Singers and musicians, on the other hand, make their money from the record sales. That was an important lesson I learnt from Cyril Shane, who was one of the nicest but meanest men I've ever met. He used to bring a six-penny carton of milk to the office every day and, when he went home, if there was any milk left he took it with him. How mean can you get?

But Cyril was also a very smart operator. I remember turning an average song called 'Come On In' by a session group named Peanuts into a hit because I got it played four times a week on the Radio Two breakfast show introduced by Terry Wogan. It was one of the most popular radio programmes of the time and I got the song so many plugs on it partly because the producer of the show, Colin Chandler, loved the song. But there was another reason. Chandler used to make kipper ties – all the rage in the 1960s – and every time I visited him I bought at least four ties. I'd learnt from my days with Izzy Mintz that you have to speculate to accumulate.

Anyhow I was well pleased with my success but all that Cyril Shane said about it was 'How many of our past hits have they been playing?' 'Who cares?' I said. 'It's the new hits we have to plug.' 'No Eric,' he replied, 'remember the Performing Rights money, that's where the profit is.' And he was right. Irving Berlin went maybe thirty years without writing a song but he was still making a fortune out of the hundreds of hits written when he was a young man.

It was an important part of my musical education but, although Cyril was only interested in the old hits, there was another man I knew nothing about who was definitely impressed by the number of plays our records were getting. He was Don Arden, a powerful wheeler-dealer manager-agent who had monster successful groups like The Love Affair, Small Faces and The Move. Don Arden's image as the Al Capone of the pop business was underlined by a story I was told about a dispute about The Small Faces. When their lead singer Steve Marriott, my old mate from those Denmark Street days, left to go solo his spot went to Rod Stewart and Stewart and the Small Faces somehow became involved with another manager named Billy Gaff. Arden wasn't pleased. He decided the Small Faces were still his and, with two of his henchmen, he visited Gaff at his office on the third floor of a building in Knightsbridge. When Billy refused to relinquish the group the henchmen held him out of the window by his legs until he changed his mind.

Anyway, he'd lost some of his power and now had fewer groups but one of them was Judas Jump whose publishers just happened to be our company. Arden couldn't believe how much air-time the group was receiving on every radio station, even though the records were not selling in the shops. He made enquiries and discovered the man responsible for all that promotion was a young record-pusher called Eric Hall.

When Roy Wood of The Move contacted Don Arden to discuss a plan for them to get together again with a whole new set-up, he decided that perhaps yours truly was the man who could help get the idea off the ground. It proved to be the start of another important era in my life and yet another new direction. I'd worked for a record company-cum-radio station, then a song writing-cum-publishing company and now I was entering the field of manager-cum-agent which, as you all now know, would become a vital part of my life when I eventually left the music business.

Chapter Four

r oy Wood, he of the pale face and the whiskers, had come up with the idea of forming a new group called Electric Light Orchestra to run alongside The Move, who had gone cold for a few years, and approached Don Arden to renew their association.

On the strength of my success with Judas Jump and The Hollies, Don decided to bring me in. But instead of approaching me directly he went around the houses by getting his son David to invite me to lunch at a well-known West End restaurant and club called Jack Isow's.

Incidentally Isow's was the favourite eating places of that great comedian Tommy Cooper who, apart from being one of the funniest English comedians ever in my opinion, also ran my old boss Cyril Shane a close second in the meanest-man stakes. He used to sit in the bar at Isow's for hours on his own and when the barman asked if he wanted a drink he'd constantly refuse. But, as soon as someone else arrived at the bar, recognized him and offered him a drink he'd immediately reply in that gravelly voice of his: 'Thank you very much, I'll have a large Scotch.'

But, back to my lunch with David. He told me that he and his father were getting together with Roy Wood again and that they wanted me as their promotion chief. He gave me a tape of a new track they were thinking of releasing called 'Tonight' and when I played it and first heard that great sound of 'I'll be over tonight' and all the boom, boom, boom I didn't need any persuading. It was what I call good old-fashioned melodic pop and I knew I could sell it big.

We had a meeting with Roy Wood, Jeff Lynne, Bev Bevan and Rick Price, the four original members of The Move who were left after Carl Wayne, the lead singer, had gone solo – not the smartest move anyone has made in the music business. Carl thought that when The Move had a hit it was his voice selling the record but, in fact, it was Roy Wood's music and lyrics that were the key to success. Carl stayed with Don Arden for a while as a solo artist – I remember trying to sell a record called 'Maybe God's Got Something Up His Sleeve' which got plenty of plays but hardly sold a copy – while Wood was still writing hits for The Move, creating the ELO and contemplating forming a group to be called Wizzard.

Although I hadn't taken too much notice when Don and David had been talking about the ELO – I was still captivated with the idea of promoting The Move – I soon became much more enthusiastic after attending a meeting with Roy and the rest of the group at Don Arden's office off Berkeley Square, when they played some ELO and Wizzard demo tapes which blew my brains. The ELO number, with all those cellos and violins, was 'Roll Over Beethoven' and The Wizzard song was 'See My Baby Jive'. I couldn't believe what I was hearing and I knew immediately they would both be smash hits. Suddenly Don Arden was being inundated with requests for the groups to do world tours but obviously it was impossible because they couldn't divide themselves into three. Something had to give although for a time all three groups, The Move, ELO and Wizzard, were monster successes.

There was an internal split as Jeff Lynne, who had taken over as vocalist, and Roy Wood were not quite seeing eye to eye and it was decided eventually that they would do a deal. This time, it was Jeff not Roy who came out of it ahead of the game. Wood was convinced

ELO would be only a short-term success and that Wizzard would, thanks to his songwriting ability, go on making hits for ever so he took Wizzard, saying almost dismissively to Lynne, 'You can have ELO.' But, as we now know, it was ELO that went from strength to strength while Wizzard disappeared into obscurity after only a few more hits. Although we were still handling all three groups and I was still getting them plenty of plays and publicity, I don't think the split helped the mood in the camp.

I'm glad to say I had no problems with Don Arden, not even when yet another approach was made to me – this time by Roy Featherstone, the top man with EMI. But I was soon to discover that Roy thought he'd got a problem with Don for making me an offer I couldn't refuse or, in my case, couldn't understand.

I should have known that Roy, despite his title as managing director at EMI, was worried about Don when I picked up the phone in my office and heard him whisper, 'Is that you Eric? Can you talk?' He managed to let me know he wanted to meet me and booked a table at Giovanni's, where he told me of the new plans EMI had for their record section. In the past they had used different labels for different types of music, Colombia, Parlophone and boom, boom, boom but in future they were going to put all the records under one umbrella, known simply as EMI.

They were going to launch the label with a new group called Blue Mink, which consisted of well-known session musicians like Roger Cook and Madelaine Bell, and a song called 'Melting Pot'. They would then push their others stars, like Cliff Richard and Cilla Black and they wanted me as their promotions manager.

Roy asked if I was interested in getting involved. Was he sure? I was still feeling like the kid selling rosettes for five bob and he wanted me to look after some of the top names in the world of pop music. But I'd learnt a few wrinkles from men like Don Arden and Cyril Shane and my monster mate Tommy Scott who was the in-house record producer at Major Minor Records. I hung back a bit then said: 'I'll join on one condition. You'll have to sign Queen for the new label.'

Now I'm not being smart and pretending I was the only person in the music business who'd heard of Queen. They were like a young footballer who every manager knows about but none of them are quite sure how high to go in the bidding. I'd seen them and so had every other manager, agent and record label representative. Queen were obviously going to be big and EMI already had the music publishing rights to the group, who were on the circuit in the south but had not yet gone national. I was merely trying to make sure they got the record rights as well so that they owned the whole package. Anyone listening to our conversation must have thought we were talking about King Kong because while I was calling Queen 'monster, monster' Roy was using his own catchphrase, 'frightening, frightening', which in his language means awesome.

Anyhow, Roy said he'd let me have an answer soon and, sure enough, he rang back two days later to arrange another meeting. When he arrived this time he didn't have to say 'frightening' because he really looked it.

'Have you told Don Arden about our meeting?' he asked. I assured him I hadn't and asked why he wanted to know. 'Because he's threatened to shoot me for trying to poach you from him,' said Roy. I told him he was being a schmuck and he eventually calmed down enough to tell me that Queen would be signed and the job was mine. He added that I would be Queen's personal promotion man until they got a number one or at least a respectable hit and if they didn't get one fairly soon I'd get the sack.

I'm not sure if he was getting his revenge but I was half expecting to be on my way back to Don Arden when their first release, 'Keep Yourself Alive' was a total flop. I got loads of air-time for them, including a half-hour spot on the BBC TV show *The Old Grey Whistle Test*, but the record just didn't appeal.

Luckily we hit a Top Ten spot with their next release, 'Seven Seas Of Rhye' in March 1974, so I kept my job and the chance to meet and work with some of the legends of the pop world over the next decade.

Chapter Five

my involvement with Queen soon became more than just a working relationship between recording artists and record promoter. They soon began to rely on me to arrange much of their personal lives for them and we became great friends. But I didn't realize just what an effect I was having on Freddie Mercury, the lead singer and star of the group.

No-one who ever met Freddie could ever be left in any doubt about his sexual preferences. He was probably the most extrovert, camp, gay person I've ever met. But I'd never really worried about that, didn't even give it a thought really. As far as I was concerned he was great company and an absolute genius when it came to writing, performing and recording songs. So it came as a bit of a shock, to say the least, to discover that the song that was to become the group's second major hit was about me and an even more monster surprise to discover that Freddie had written it as a love song for me.

It had not taken long for me to become known at EMI as Mr Extravagant. I always had a fleet of luxury cars on hand to chauffeur my clients to gigs, recording studios, restaurants or whatever. In my office I had a cocktail cabinet – old-fashioned word I know but I'm an old-fashioned Jewish boy – which always contained the very best champagne for my guests. And, what will come as something of a surprise to those who have only known me since I switched to becoming a sports agent, I had the most beautiful head of hair you've ever seen. It was long and permed, in the style known as the Lamour which was all the rage in the mid-1970s.

As Queen were now one of the company's best artists when Freddie rang one morning in 1974 to say he wanted to see me alone in my office I was not going to refuse. When he arrived he said to me: 'Eric, I want you to listen to the song I have written which we are planning to release as our next single.' He proceeded to play this wonderful track called 'Killer Queen', the words of which went some-thing like 'He keeps Moet & Chandon in his fancy cabinet. He has long hair just like Marie Antionette'. But at the time I wasn't taking much notice of the words. I could just tell it was a fantastic song. So I told Freddie, 'It's amazing, it's going to be a monster hit.' 'But you haven't listened to it Eric,' said Freddie.

'Of course I have, you schmuck, I just told you I love it.'

'But what about the lyric?'

'What's with this lyric stuff?' I knew this wasn't the age of Cole Porter or Jerome Kern. No-one listened to words anymore.

'Please Eric, listen to the lyrics,' said Freddie.

So I listened and it finally dawned on me what he was talking about. 'That person in the song sounds familiar,' I said. 'Yes Eric, I've written the song for you. I am in love with you but you are driving me crazy. You are killing me because you don't respond. That's why I've called it "Killer Queen",' he confessed. 'I'm the Queen and you're the killer.'

I knew Freddie had as much chance of making love to me as I had of making love to Brigitte Bardot, but he still didn't seem to under-stand that. Obviously my appearance had given him entirely the wrong idea about me.

I have never before told anyone this story and I only do so now for the sake of setting the record straight about the relationship between Freddie and me. I did love him but in a way that brothers love each other. I felt really close to him mentally but that was as far as it could ever go, so I became even more embarrassed some time later when Freddie told me that he wanted to spend the night in my bedroom with me.

'Look, you know how I feel Freddie. It's just not on,' I told him.

'No, I don't mean I want to sleep with you.' he said. 'I just want to sit and watch while you're asleep,' he said.

Oh yeah, I thought, is he sure? I wasn't born yesterday. But, he pleaded with me so much I eventually agreed he could stay in my room as long as he sat in the armchair and never moved all night. He promised he would and, I have to say, he kept his word and never bothered me again after that. 'You are out of my system now,' he said, which came as a great relief to me even though I still regarded him as one of my closest friends. It was not long after this, however, that I found I could no longer get through to Freddie. I knew the group was working on their next album and, naturally, I wanted to know how they were progressing and if they had a song on it they could release as their next single. But no matter how many times I tried to get through, I could never pin them down. 'Oh Eric, Freddie will call you back later,' I was told constantly but he never did and neither did any other member of the group. I began to think that not only had he got me out of his system sexually but that he'd decided to bomb me altogether – which would have been a disaster considering I was Queen's record promoter.

Happily, just as I was getting really paranoid about it and starting to tell myself 'Well, I've got Cliff Richard and Cilla Black and plenty of other stars, what do I care?' which was nonsense because I really did care, out of the blue I finally received a call from Freddie.

'It's time for another meeting, Eric,' he told me.

'Where have you been? Have I upset you? What's the problem?' I asked.

'Of course you haven't upset me and there's no problem. We've just been busy. But I'm now ready to let you hear our next single so can I come to your office, play the record and then take you to lunch?'

Could he just! He could even watch me sleep again if he wanted to, that's how relieved I was. Within half an hour he was in my office with the tape. It wasn't like it is now with CDs and all that stuff, we just used an old-fashioned reel-to-reel Grundig tape recorder. Freddie set it up, hit the play button and out came one of the most fantastic song I'd ever heard, 'Bohemian Rhapsody'.

'Mama, just killed a man. Put a gun against his head, pulled the trigger now he's dead.' It had only been on thirty seconds and I was already crying. But almost nine minutes later the record was still playing and I was totally bewildered.

'Freddie, it's fantastic but we've got a major problem here,' I told him.

'What are you talking about?' he asked.

So I had to explain that the record lasted nine minutes-ish and I had LPs that were shorter than that. The problem was that every radio station in those days had what they called a play-list of fifty records which they played daily. It consisted of about 60 per cent of the current Top Fifty, maybe 30 per cent were what you might call raves from the grave and only 10 per cent were new releases. Why would the DJs and programme producers take one record that lasted nine minutes when they could have three that lasted only three minutes each? I told Freddie that although I was the greatest record plugger in the business, which without being being-headed I knew was a fact, it was going to be tough pushing this one.

I asked if he could cut the playing time of the record without losing any of the impact and he told me he could probably get it down to seven minutes. So I moved into my selling routine with what I knew was probably the best pop record I'd ever handle but also the hardest to get plays with.

Luckily, by this time, I'd become very good friends with Doreen Davies, the programme controller for Radio One – not a bad contact to have. Although she didn't actually choose the weekly play-list, Doreen held a meeting every Tuesday morning with the producers and DJs of all the Radio One programmes to choose the following week's list for each show. So it was vitally important to get her on my side as soon as possible. Normally she was a tough lady to get hold of and even tougher to get a meeting with. But I had her private number and got through immediately.

'Can I see you Doreen?' I asked.

'You know how busy I am Eric, won't one of my producers be able to help you?'

'No, I've got Queen's latest record and I think you should hear it before anyone else does.'

'OK. Can you come around now? We'll have a cup of coffee and listen to the tape,' she said.

Any promotions man would have given a fortune to get a response like that and it showed just how important Queen were at the time. I arrived, put on the tape and within thirty seconds she had had the same reaction as I had and we were both crying into our coffee. But soon I could also see Doreen beginning to look uncomfortable. 'When does it end?' she kept asking me. 'Any second now,' I'd reply, but the minutes ticked away. At the end she confirmed my fears. 'I love it,' she said, 'and I'll certainly let all the DJs hear it, but I can't honestly guarantee you'll get many plays on this one Eric.'

It so happened that we had met on a Tuesday morning just before her weekly listings meeting and I returned to my office feeling a bit down. Even though EMI hadn't even got a release date for the record yet, they hadn't discussed it even, I knew I could have a monster, monster hit on my hands if only I could get it across to the record-buying public. I was still pondering over the problem when, at four o'clock that afternoon, my phone rang and it was David 'Diddy' Hamilton, then one of Radio One's top DJs.

'Eric, I've just heard the new Queen record. When is it going to be released?' he asked.

'Why, do you like it?'

'I'm crazy about it and as soon as it's out I'm going to make it my record of the week,' he said.

That was the best news I could have been given because when a Radio One DJ decided on a record of the week every other DJ was automatically obliged to play the same record at least once. It meant that in the first week of release I was guaranteed a minimum fifteen plays on Radio One alone.

As soon as I received that news, I immediately went to Radio Luxembourg, then one of the biggest influences on the British record market, to see another of my top DJ contacts, Kid Jensen, now known as David Jensen. I was one of the few promoters who took the trouble to pay personal visits to Luxembourg, which they appreciated, and I figured I might get some good plays from them. As soon as Kid Jensen had heard 'Bohemian Rhapsody' and had recovered from the seven-minute shock, he decided to make it his Power Play record of the week. That meant the station was going to play it six times a night.

I knew then my problems were over. If the listeners were as impressed as the disc jockeys there was nothing that could stop it hitting number one. It did and stayed in the charts for a spectacular seventeen weeks. I can also inform those Queen fans, who may not have known the original recording was nine minutes long, that they didn't really miss anything with the final seven-minute version. Freddie and Brian May did such a good job in the editing studio you would never have known it had been cut.

Chapter Six

I've been asked many times just what the 'real' Freddie Mercury was like. Was the man who was such an outrageously camp personality on stage the same in his private life? I have to say the answer is yes. He was just as outrageously camp wherever he was but often, as with so many people like Freddie, that behaviour covered up an underlying shyness. He was also a person who couldn't stand being alone. Even if he was in a crowd he had to make sure someone he knew and trusted was next to him.

I had many marvellous nights out with Freddie and his friends and the one that sticks in my mind most, for a very strange reason, was a New Year's Eve dinner he threw at a West End club called Maunkberry's. Apart from Freddie and the rest of Queen the party included Elton John, Rod Stewart and Britt Ekland as well as many other stars I didn't know personally.

Anyone who knows me well will vouch for the fact that when I do go out drinking I need to spend a lot of time having wee-wees and, sure enough, as midnight drew closer I needed to spend a penny yet again. I thought I had time but as I stood at the urinal I heard the boing-boing of Big Ben and suddenly the New Year was upon us and I could hear the strains of 'Auld Lang Syne' coming from the restaurant.

It so happened, however, that I wasn't alone in the toilet because another of Freddie's guests was standing next to me. And as we finished our tiddles he turned to me, gave me a hug and a kiss on the cheek and wished me a Happy New Year. I suddenly realized it was Christopher Reeve. I couldn't help saying to him: 'Who is going to believe me when I tell them I saw in the New Year with Superman in a toilet?' I haven't seen Christopher since but I often think of that night and of the brave battle he's put up since the accident which left him crippled. And every New Year I say a special little prayer that one day he will fully recover.

I also remember having a meal with Freddie at a well-known Chelsea restaurant where we were discussing business when a huge brute of man started hurling insults at him from across the room.

'Look, it's that bloke from Queen, the big poof,' he kept shouting.

I had never before seen Freddie lose his temper, normally he just camped it up even more if people had a go, but this time he started to get all butch-ish and had a go back.

'Calm down,' I told him. 'Just ignore the schmuck and he'll shut up.'

'I'm not letting him call me a poof and get away with it, I'll give him a good hiding,' said Freddie.

I was horrified. 'Are you mad! Even Joe Bugner wouldn't fight him,' I said.

'Who said anything about fighting?' replied Freddie. 'I'll invite him around for a game of cards and give him a good hiding at poker.'

I then realized he'd been having me on, but that was typical of the mercurial Mr Mercury who I still miss so much and think about whenever I hear one of his records which, I'm glad to say, are still being played regularly.

The only time we ever fell out over anything was when Freddie wanted to do a promotion video for 'Bohemian Rhapsody'. I didn't think it was necessary because after entering the charts at number thirty it went immediately up to number fifteen and then hit number one, so I couldn't see the point of any extra publicity. But in the end I gave in and agreed to Mike Mansfield, one of the top TV producers and video makers around at the time, doing the job. My main reason for agreeing was that Mike was also very cheap and I reckoned I could get the video made for as little as £500ish.

I set the deal up and planned to start filming as soon as Queen returned from a tour they were doing in Japan. But the night before they were due to fly home Freddie called me from Tokyo. 'Cancel the video session with Mike Mansfield,' he said 'we want a friend of ours named Bruce Gowers to do it.'

'But Mike is great and he's within our budget,' I said.

'Forget your budget, Bruce is the best and we want him.'

'And how much will he charge?'

'About £30,000,' said Freddie. I thought he was having me on, after all, in those days you could make a full-length movie for £30,000.

'Are you potty?' I asked, but he was deadly serious.

'Sorry Freddie, but no way can I authorize that.'

'Don't bother then, we'll pay for it ourselves,' he said and slammed down the phone.

And he did, and once again his judgement was proved to be dead right because the video was shown all over Europe and the United States and boosted the sale of 'Bohemian Rhapsody' to even greater heights. The video also won more awards than any other ever made and is still considered a classic. So I had to tell him 'You win again' and I'm glad to say we didn't stay on bad terms for very long.

Although I'd left EMI while Queen were still at the peak of their success Freddie and I remained close friends. I was privileged to be one of the few people to be allowed to see him when he was dying. As he was so ill towards the end – he kept going into a coma then recovering for a short while before having another relapse – it was decided not to allow too many visitors to his home in Holland Park.

But I actually saw him the day before he finally passed away. I held Freddie's hand and tried to assure him that everything was all right. But he knew what was happening and the last thing he said to me was 'Eric, you've been a great friend and a very important person in my life. Thank you.'

I was devastated when, less than twenty-four hours later, I received a call from the Queen office to tell me he had died. While I could never respond to him on a physical level I truly loved that man. One of my most treasured possessions is the gold disc he was awarded for 'Bohemian Rhapsody' which is now hanging on my wall at home. I have others from Cliff Richard, Wings, T-Rex and Pilot which I'm also very proud of, but this was the first and most cherished.

Each member of Queen was given a disc at a special ceremony and afterwards we went out to celebrate. By the end of the night, and after I don't know how many bottles of champagne, Freddie was very drunk and very sentimental – he could get tipsy on a wine gum. As he left to go home he said: 'This gold disc belongs to you Eric because you worked harder for it than I did.'

I told him not to be silly and to look after it. 'No, you must have it or I'll never speak to you again,' he insisted.

In the end I took it just to make sure it was safe – I thought he might leave it in a taxi or something. But the next day when I tried to return it to Freddie he still insisted it was mine and, as he was now sober and obviously meant it, I gratefully accepted the gift.

Chapter Seven

back in those long-ago days when I was a cheeky schoolboy in the north London suburb of Stamford Hill, one of my best friends was a lad named Mark Feld whom I had first met in a place we called The Schtip House. It was actually an amusement arcade but because we always went there hoping to take money away from it we made up the name Schtip House from the Jewish word Schtip, meaning 'to take'.

We were about thirteen years old and music was becoming a major factor in our lives so Mark and I went every Sunday night to a disco called El Toro in St John's Wood. It was a long hike from Stamford Hill but it was the nearest Jewish disco – I suppose it should have been called the Let My People Go-Go.

In case you are wondering what the relevance of all this is I can tell you that Mark Feld was another of my friends who changed his name. He became Marc Bolan, leader singer of T-Rex and another superstar whose path I crossed early in life.

While I was packing parcels with Elton John and meeting David Bowie and the other lads in those Denmark Street days, Mark Feld was busy writing songs and trying to break into the recording business a different way.

We still met occasionally but it was a fantastic day for both of us when, soon after I joined EMI, I bumped into Marc Bolan, as he had now become, in their headquarters. By an amazing coincidence he had just re-joined EMI after breaking from the company several years earlier to go to America. When he saw me he hugged me and asked: 'What are you doing here bubbelah?' 'I work here,' I told him. 'In fact I'm your new promotions manager.' And, I swear, Marc started to cry with joy.

I have to admit, however, that I had received an even bigger shock on meeting my old friend because he was monster, monster overweight. I don't know what he'd been up to in America but he was at least four stone heavier than when I'd last met him and for a lad of his height, or lack of it, that was just ridiculous. He had obviously become involved in the drug scene in the United States – so easily done in those days – and I was desperately worried about him, not just because he was an artist that I was being paid to promote but because he was one of my closest friends. We already had a single lined up for the group but I knew I had no chance of selling it while Marc was looking like Billy Bunter so I contacted his manager, Tony Howard. I'm glad to say he agreed with me that drastic action had to be taken, it was no good just giving Marc a diet sheet and sending him out for a jog every day. So we sent him to one of the top health farms where he was put on a crash-course diet.

In the meantime I had an idea which I thought would help get Marc back to the top of the charts. There was a very influential pop programme going out produced by Muriel Young, a good friend of mine who had been popular as a children's programme presenter but was now a top music executive with Granada Television. It was Mu, as we called her, who had turned groups like The Arrows, Bay City Rollers and many others into stars by giving them a regular series in the pop spot and I realized it was the perfect vehicle to re-launch T-Rex.

So I invited Muriel to lunch at Morton's, the famous Berkeley Square restaurant – what's the point of having an expense account if you don't spend and enjoy it – and propositioned her, so to speak. 'I hear you have an opening on the show for a group,' I said, 'and I also know in the past you've always gone for new groups. But how would you like a group that have already been superstars?' She looked puzzled until I mentioned Marc Bolan. Muriel thought about it and then said: 'I hear he's not in the best of health Eric and, as it's a children's programme, I can't really use anyone who might look as if he's on drugs.' I assured her that everything was now under control and pleaded with her to give me four to six weeks to get Marc in tip-top shape again. 'I've got some great new music for him, I've even got a great title in *Marc Time*, all I need is the vehicle to help put him back where he belongs,' I pleaded. And, God bless her, Muriel agreed to hold off choosing a group for the show until I was ready to present the new-look Bolan for her approval.

Sure enough, after six weeks, Marc was completely clear of drugs and was back to his matchstick thin self and the lovely Muriel had no hesitation in giving him the spot. It was a huge success. Not only did T-Rex storm back to the top of the charts but Marc also decided to introduce, as guest groups on the show, a whole host of new-wave bands. No-one knew it at the time, but it was the start of the punk-rock era and because Bolan was the first to bring this music onto television he became known as the Godfather of Punk.

I was delighted to be involved in helping Marc back to the top. In those teenage years he had tried modelling, poetry writing and then singing because he was totally convinced he would be a star at something. And, as his best friend in those days, I had just accepted that he would make it, although I wasn't too sure about the poetry. He used to say to me, 'Eric, I've just written a new poem. Have a listen and tell me what you think.' I'd listen and say, 'That is the biggest load of rubbish I've ever heard in my life.' Marc would just laugh and say, 'You know that and I know it but when I'm a star it will be worth a fortune.'

And he was probably right because if you listen to some of the lyrics of his biggest hits they don't make any sense either, in fact they are probably the same poems he used to read to me. His drawings were the same, the sort of stuff kids do in nursery school. But, if I'd kept them they would probably be worth millions.

Just to return to that poetry for a moment, it was typical of Marc that when his son was born he christened him Rolan. Can you believe that? Rolan Bolan. I had a go at Marc so much about the name that he later bought me a Rolex watch saying: 'You won't have to wind up that the way you've been winding me up.' Many years later I met Rolan and told him how I had ribbed his father mercilessly about giving him the name. I asked if he'd ever thought about having it changed by deed poll. 'No, he gave me the name and I'm proud of it,' he replied, which made me feel very humble.

Marc was always such a name dropper you never knew when he was serious and when he was telling downright lies. He'd often call me to say 'Gloria (that was his beautiful lady, the actress Gloria Jones) and I are having some friends around on Sunday, would you like to join us?' I'd ask what friends and he'd reply, 'Oh just David Niven, Rod Stewart, Roger Moore, Shirley Bassey, oh, and Frank Sinatra is in town and has promised to come.' This is the lad I grew up with and he's telling me Sinatra's having lunch with us. But often I'd turn up and although Ol' Blue Eyes wasn't there sure enough Niven, Stewart, Moore, Bassey or whoever would be there so I was never sure when to believe him.

I'm delighted to say that Marc stayed with that Granada show for a couple of years and it was voted the top pop show on television – well, by me anyhow. We also produced many major hits together for EMI. One I recall was 'New York City' which contains the lyric 'Have you ever seen a woman walking down the street with a frog in her hand in New York City.' See what I mean about his lyrics?

It was moving well up the charts and we were on our third *Top Of The Pops* with it. I always believed we should try and do something different on every *TOTP* appearance to keep interest alive in the record so during the Wednesday rehearsal for the Thursday show on our third visit I said to Marc: 'You know that bit about the lady walking down the road with a frog in her hand, why don't we get someone to dress up as a frog and dance around while you sing the song?' He replied, 'That's a sensational idea, who can we get to do it?'

Of course, everyone looked at me. I was lumbered but, being an egomaniac I didn't argue too much. I was going to be on television even though I was inside a frog-suit and no-one knew it was me. We did the show and it went very well. In fact, it went so well we were asked to repeat the performance when we appeared on another show, this time for London Weekend on their *Saturday Scene* show which went out live. Warren Breech, the producer, had seen *Top Of The Pops* and phoned me the following day. 'Everything set for Saturday?'

'Sure, the car is laid on and they'll be there such-and-such a time.'

'By the way Eric, that frog routine was brilliant. If we pay an extra fee can we get whoever played the frog to do it for us?'

'You liked it then?'

'Yes, sensational.'

'More than sensational I'd say, Warren.'

'Well, who was it then?'

'It was me.'

'Right, then you'll do it for us?'

'Depends on how much you're paying.'

'But you're the promotion man, you're getting the publicity.'

'I know, but you said you're paying so I get paid.'

'OK, but no credit, just Eric The Frog.'

'Done.'

As a result I ended up appearing in a Royal Variety Children's Show at Drury Lane in front of Princess Margaret. Marc Bolan was invited to appear and, under no pressure from me I assure you, he chose to sing 'New York City'. Warren Breech was again producing the show so naturally the frog had to be included. However I was told in no uncertain terms that when Princess Margaret was presented to the performers after the show I could stand in line but I had to keep the frog's head on.

But, what the hell I thought, they can't throw me in the Tower can they? So when the Princess got to me I whipped off the frog's head, stuck it under my arm and shook hands with her. I don't think Warren ever forgave me for pulling that stroke but I just couldn't resist it.

Chapter Eight

Yom Kippur is a very important date in the Jewish calendar. It is the day when we atone for our sins and reflect on life – and sometimes death. In my case it is one very special death that I think about when Jewish New Year – the week leading up to Yom Kippur – arrives. It was at the start of a New Year, on 17 September 1977, that Marc Bolan was killed in a car crash.

It was the same year that Elvis Presley died but whereas I hated Presley, not as a person because I never met him but as a performer, I was as close to Marc as I had been to anyone outside my family. We grew up together, shared our teenage secrets and ambitions and had reached the stage where we were a formidable team with his talent for making records and mine for selling them. He had overcome his weight and drug problems and there was nothing but further success for him on the horizon when he was so cruelly snatched from us.

His death came as an even bigger shock to me because in the weeks prior to his death I had actually been living with Marc. His lady Gloria had gone to New York to make some recordings of her own and as he hated being alone and also couldn't drive he asked me to move in to both keep him company and act as his chauffeur. It was no hardship for me because I was living with my mum in Loughton at this time so it was easier for me to be in central London and I also enjoyed being with Marc – in many ways we acted as if were still schoolkids. We had a fabulous two weeks but when Gloria returned it was clear I would move out.

We had planned a welcome home meal at Morton's for the night she returned to London. Gloria's brother Richard drove to the airport to collect her while Marc and I got things organized at the restaurant. We had a lovely evening and during the meal I mentioned that I would be going back to Loughton. This upset Marc who insisted that I continued to stay at their place. I pretended to agree but while he wasn't looking I had a quick word with Gloria, told her I was sure she and Marc didn't want me around – especially on their first night back together – and said I'd tell Marc I was going for a wee-wee but instead I would slip out by the back door and get a taxi home.

That's what I did and the next morning I was up early and in my car on the way to the office when I heard a news bulletin: 'Pop star Marc Bolan is dead. His car, driven by his girlfriend's brother, hit a tree in central London in the early hours of the morning.' It seemed that Marc had died instantly while Gloria and Richard were badly injured but survived. I went numb and had to stop the car. All I could think of was that if I had stayed on I would have driven them home and he might still be alive. I don't think I've ever really recovered from the shock of that day and every year 17 September is a very sad day for me.

It was a particularly sad day last year as it was the twentieth anniversary of his death. A memorial service was held at Golders Green, to which all of his friends and fellow artists turned up and Rolan came over from America. There was one humorous event on an otherwise sombre day when someone saw Rolan and said, 'I'd have recognized you anywhere as Marc's boy.' I couldn't help butting in and saying, 'Are you sure? Marc was Jewish, white, seven stone and about 5 ft 6 in tall while Rolan is 6 ft 2 in, about 14 stone and black.'

There was one other amazing sequel to Marc's death which few people believe but I swear is emmes (that's the Jewish word for 'true, on my life' and is not to be used lightly).

Marc had been due to appear on *Top Of The Pops* just a few days after Gloria had arrived home and he asked me to take his favourite jacket to the dry cleaners so he could wear it on the show. Naturally I never gave it a thought again after his death until about five years later when I found the dry cleaning ticket in a draw I was clearing out. At first I couldn't remember why I had such a ticket, and then it dawned on me that if was for Marc's jacket. I didn't think there was any chance it would still be there but, on the off chance, I called in at the shop to ask. The manager went away and ten minutes later appeared with the jacket which I still have.

People never believe that story but it's monster, monster true. And so is the story of the stroke I pulled as a song plugger when I was bidding to get a number one hit over Christmas. That's like winning an Oscar for record promoters and the number I was pushing was 'I Wish It Could Be Christmas Every Day' by Wizzard. It's now considered a classic but it was proving very difficult for me to get plays with when it first came out in November 1973.

I was desperate to get it on one particular programme – *Family Favourites* – on Radio One and Two because I knew if the kids wanted it for Christmas it was a guaranteed hit. The producer of the show was a man named Jack Dabbs who was harder to get hold of than the Scarlet Pimpernel. No matter how hard I tried, my route to him always seemed to be blocked. Eventually I was told by one of his assistants that the reason he couldn't see me the following morning was that he was taking his nephews to see Father Christmas at Allders store in Croydon. They say necessity is the mother of invention and I invented a real beauty this time.

I went to Moss Bros that afternoon and hired a Santa outfit. I arrived at Allders early the following morning, had a chat with the resident Father Christmas, told him what I was up to and bribed him to let me stand in for him as soon as I saw Jack Dabbs and the children in the queue. He was happy to make a few extra quid – even Santas have to make a living – and the switch was made. I asked Jack's nephews what they wanted for Christmas and guaranteed them they would get everything on the list if they did me a favour. I gave them a copy of the Wizzard record and told them to tell Uncle Jack what a wonderful song it was. They didn't have a clue why Santa wanted this favour but I got quite heavy with them and they went along with it – what kid's going to risk upsetting him! Eventually Jack was driven crazy by their constant chatter about the record and asked them where it came from. He couldn't believe it when they said that Santa Claus had given it to them but in the end I finally contacted him and owned up that it was me. It could have back-fired but Jack was so amazed by my audacity that he played it on his show and it entered the charts at number six, making all my efforts well worthwhile.

While it was usually me amazing the people I was chasing to plug records, sometimes it was the other way around and I was the one who got the shock. One of the men who never failed to surprise me was the wonderful Jimmy Saville who is what we Jews would call a mensch – a real gent.

His programme *Saville's Travels* was one of the top radio programmes during my time with EMI. It was so popular any record played by Jimmy was almost guaranteed to be a hit so we promotion boys were always desperate to take him to lunch and try and sell one of our latest products. In fact, he was so popular he was like the NHS – he had a six-month waiting list. I remember one occasion when it was my turn to take Jimmy out. I picked him up in the limo and told him I'd booked us in at Les Ambassadeurs in Park Lane, one of London's most expensive restaurants.

'Do me a favour Eric, do you mind if I take you somewhere that's even better,' said Jimmy. 'Even better than Les Ambassadeurs, where are we going Buckingham Palace?' I asked. To my amazement Jimmy gave the driver instructions to take us to King's Cross. We stopped at a little greasy-spoon cafe where, I have to say, the food was excellent and the welcome very friendly.

'I really get fed up with those snotty-nosed big restaurants and it's great to be able to relax in a place like this, don't you agree?' said Jimmy. I looked at the bill and definitely agreed. It had cost me about four quid instead of the £400 I would have forked out in Park Lane.

Chapter Nine

the variety of the stars I handled during my time with EMI was never more clearly illustrated than by the gap that existed between Cliff Richard and The Sex Pistols. It was definitely a case of saints and sinners when it came to handling these two entirely different acts.

The mild-mannered Cliff would never upset anyone and was brave enough to stand up for his Christian beliefs at a time when it was not always popular to do so. Johnny Rotten and The Sex Pistols were, by comparison, the Devil's disciples. They were new on the pop scene and I have to admit I hated their music but I appreciated their potential. I was always a ballads man myself. I'd sit at home playing Frank Sinatra, Frankie Laine, Dorothy Squires or even Doris Day. I loved great lyrics and couldn't understand why anyone would make a record on which the words were completely unintelligible. But, no matter what my personal feelings about a particular group, I was paid to push their records and that's what I did with them all, including The Sex Pistols.

The first record they made that I was required to promote was 'Anarchy In The UK' in December 1976. They were just beginning to become well known at this time but they were not exactly household names. But that was all about to change thanks to a show called *Today* with Bill Grundy on Thames Television.

I was very friendly with the producer, Mike Housego, and we had arranged to have a member of Queen on to plug their latest record on what Mike called his 'pop spot' in the programme. But it turned out there was a problem with the Musicians' Union over the Queen video that was going to be shown and suddenly on the day of the show Mike was desperate for a replacement. 'What about Cliff Richard?' he asked me. I had to turn that idea down because Cliff's latest release wasn't yet in the shops so there was no use me plugging it. 'Well how about this new group you've got, The Sex Pistols, they've got a new release haven't they?' asked Mike. 'Are you potty?' I replied. 'If you have them on the programme live anything can happen.'

But in the end my need for a good plug overtook my worries about what might be said and I agreed to call them. It so happened they were rehearsing at a pub in Hammersmith when I contacted their manager, the colourful character Malcolm McLaren. 'I've booked you on to the *Today* show but you've got to get there within the next couple of hours,' I told him. Now Malcolm, despite his name, is a lovely Jewish boy like myself and his reaction was exactly the same as mine had been.

'Are you mad, Monster?' he said. 'That bloke Grundy will goad them into saying something stupid and we'll be in trouble again.' I knew what he was talking about. Bill Grundy was reknowned for being very controversial and for enjoying very long, liquid lunches which only fuelled his abrasiveness on air.

But the clock was ticking away and I gave Malcolm the biggest routine ever. 'It will be a great plug for the group and the record,' I told him.

'But it only goes out in the London area,' he replied.

'Don't worry,' I told him. 'This could be just the plug we need to get the record off the ground.' Eventually he cracked and agreed to let them appear. But he made certain stipulations. 'I want them picked up in a limo and I want champagne and smoked salmon sandwiches laid on for them,' he told me. That was no problem but I did find it rather ironic that a group that were supposed to be representing the punk people of the world and were worried about their so-called 'street cred' should be demanding such upper-class luxuries.

I got them to the studio on time and made Housego promise me that he would ensure that Grundy didn't pull any strokes. I also warned the lads in the group, saying: 'Whatever happens, don't let Grundy goad you into saying anything stupid, just talk about the record.' But from the beginning I sensed there was going to be trouble. Grundy wasn't interested in the record, only in trying to get the boys to be outrageous because that's what he expected them to be.

'Go on, say something that will shock me,' he kept saying to them. They did their best to keep their tempers but, in the end, Steve Jones cracked and called Grundy a dirty b*****d and other words to that effect. Of course, it caused a sensation and the newspapers were full of it for days. But it didn't have the effect Grundy was expecting. Instead of making him a star it got him the sack from the show for breaking his promise. And, instead of making The Sex Pistols look stupid, as he'd hoped, it turned them into overnight celebrities and made sure the record was a hit.

Although I didn't like their music I never had any real bother with the band. They were not the guilty party in that incident and I found that most of the time they would co-operate with my plans to promote them. Although they tried to put on a tough image it was all an act. They were pussycats when the crunch came – I even saw little Marc Bolan frighten them once.

He and I were leaving my office just as they were arriving. 'Hello lads,' I said. 'Do you know Marc Bolan?'

Now Marc was a great lover of flamboyant ties and was wearing one of his huge kipper ties on this occasion. And The Sex Pistols started taking the mickey out of him about it. 'You're about ten years out of date mate, just like your music,' said one of them. And another of them, I think it was Sid Vicious, produced a penknife and said, 'Let me cut it down to size for you,' and waved the knife at Marc's tie. I could sense Marc's anger rising and tried to pull him away but he fronted the guy and said: 'If you are looking for trouble you've found it. One more word and I'll kick you straight down those stairs.' Immediately the attitude of The Sex Pistols changed. 'Sorry Marc, didn't mean it, just having a laugh' they said and, as far as I was concerned, yet another myth bit the dust. What a contrast between them and the fabulous Cliff Richard.

I saw Cliff lose his cool only once, and that was a very polite admonishment to someone in a restaurant who refused to wait until he'd finished his meal before asking for an autograph. Most of the time Sir Cliff, as he is now, would go out of his way to do things for his adoring fans and he refused to let his Christian standards drop even if it cost him money.

He made a record called 'Honky Tonk Angel'. The disc had been pressed and I had sent copies to every disc jockey and record reviewer when I received a call from his manager Peter Gormley. 'Have you sent out the review copies yet?' he asked. I told him they'd been out for two days. 'Get them all back, the record has to be scrapped,' he told me. I couldn't believe my ears. 'What are you talking about? Everyone I have spoken to loves it. Noel Edmonds has already decided to make it his record of the week and it's a guaranteed number one, possibly his best ever hit,' I told him. But he was adamant and explained that Cliff had mentioned to some of his religious friends what his next record was called and had been devastated to discover that a honky-tonk angel was another name for a prostitute. 'He can't possibly make money out of glamorizing such a person,' he told me.

So instead of plugging a sure-fire hit I was given the job of making sure that not one copy of the record was ever allowed to remain in circulation. I didn't even keep one for myself, which is a great shame because I reckon it would now be worth a fortune.

My other great memory of Cliff concerns a message that was waiting for me when I returned from a trip to Marbella. It was from Peter Gormley, who has since sadly died after managing Cliff from the very start of his career.

It said that Peter, Cliff and Bruce Welch, one of the famous Shadows group who was then producing Cliff's records, wanted to take me to dinner at La Loggia restaurant in the Edgware Road to discuss a promotion idea. I was only too happy to go but when I arrived I discovered not only were Cliff, Bruce and Peter there but Peter Vernon, the official EMI photographer, was also present. I had no idea what was happening until Cliff said: 'Right lads, let's do it before we eat.' He then produced a gold disc presented to him for an LP called 'I'm Nearly Famous' which I'd promoted and had gone into the Top Ten album lists all over the world. We had also taken a single from the album called 'Miss You Nights' which was not only a massive hit over here but was also the first record Cliff made which reached the top end of the American charts.

The record had heralded the start of Cliff's change of image from what I'd call the Eurovision Song Contest singer to the performer of great ballads which he has become since then. I knew that Cliff had appreciated the support I'd given him within EMI to make that change which the hierarchy in the compnany had been against.

My argument had been that if it failed he could always go back to the old Cliff routine and wouldn't be any worse off. But I didn't expect to be presented with the 'I'm Nearly Famous' gold disc or the card that went with it which read: 'To Eric-I'll-send-a-limo-Hall. You are famous with us' and was signed by Cliff and Bruce. It was a very special moment for me.

Chapter Ten

One of my favourite English songs of all time was a number written by Ted Heath – no, not the politician but the man who was one of this country's greatest-ever big band leaders. It was a wartime hit called 'I Haven't Said Thanks For That Lovely Weekend'. It was my memory of that song that led to me signing another group for EMI and another number one hit record.

My boss, Bob Mercer, called me into his office one day and said: 'We've been offered this new group and although we are over budget for the year I'd like your opinion as head of promotions about whether we should sign them.' He handed me a tape and I looked at the label which read: 'Pilot. Managed by Tim and Nick Heath.' I knew they were the sons of the great Ted Heath so I said: 'Yes, I've heard that group and they are brilliant. Sign them.' So they did and it wasn't until a week later when I finally met Tim and Nick in my office that I actually heard the tape.

'I've recommended the company to sign Pilot so I might as well hear what they sound like,' I said. It gave them a good laugh but when I heard the tape I knew immediately that by a sheer fluke I'd picked a winner. The tape included the songs 'Magic', 'January' and 'Just A Smile' which were all absolutely up my street. We decided to push 'Just A Smile' first and I started ringing all my television and radio contacts. One show where I desperately wanted a play was *Supersonic* which appeared on ITV on a Saturday and was produced by my good friend Mike Mansfield so I figured I'd have no problem. But when I called his office on the Wednesday I was told he was in the south of France and wouldn't be back for a week. 'He's phoning his programme instructions in on Thursday,' his secretary told me. I asked where he was staying and she told me it was the Carlton Hotel in Cannes.

I immediately booked a flight to France and arrived on Thursday morning with the Pilot tape. I called Mike's room from reception and told him, 'I've got a record I want on your show this week.'

'Can't it wait until next week Eric, I've almost filled all the spots for this week.'

'But I've come all this way for you to hear it,' I said.

'What do you mean?' asked Mike. 'Where are you?' When I told him I was downstairs he was totally knocked out and invited me up.

'Why have you come all this way, what's so special about this group?' he asked.

'I'm here because this group is monster, monster,' I said.

'You mean they're ugly?'

'No, they are going to be monster, monster huge,' I told him. I don't know why I've always used that phrase but that's where the title of this book was born. It worked because Mike was so impressed when he heard the track that he put it on the show and it was a hit, although not quite as big as the follow-up records 'Magic' and 'January'.

Pilot never did become quite as monster, monster as I'd predicted because, like many groups of that era, there was soon a split in the camp as the members chased individual stardom.

Another group that I was involved with from its inception was Wings. I received a call in the autumn of 1977 from a man called Brian Brolly, who was Paul McCartney's manager and also later handled the brilliant Andrew Lloyd Webber – so he was no mug. 'Can you meet us at Paul's office in Soho Square to hear his latest record?' he asked.

When Paul had returned to EMI, who had recorded all the original Beatles hits on the Parlophone label, he'd asked for me personally to promote Wings' records. This was a great honour for me so I was excited at the prospect of hearing a new McCartney composition. When I arrived at the office Paul was there with Brian and a man called Alan Crowder, who is currently Paul's manager and who asks me every year if I can get him Cup Final tickets.

Wings had already had a couple of successful records, including 'Silly Love Songs', and when Brian put on the new one I was expecting a similar sound. What I heard instead was this wailing noise that I instantly hated. Just then the lovely Linda McCartney arrived – I'm so sad that I am writing this only weeks after her tragic death – and she drawled 'Hello Eric' in that sexy voice of hers. 'What do you think of the new record?' 'I think they played it at the wrong speed,' I replied and then realized that no-one had found my joke very amusing.'No it's all about the Mull of Kintyre and it's a song for Paul's Scottish ancestors and will make a great Christmas number,' said Linda.

I reckoned it would make a better New Year number with all that bagpipe stuff but I agreed to put the whole EMI promotion team behind the song in a bid to get the coveted Christmas number one spot. Naturally, because it was a Paul McCartney number, there was no problem getting plenty of air-time and it not only hit the top but stayed in the charts for seventeen weeks. I have to admit I did get to like it after three or four plays but it's still not one of my favourites.

'Mull Of Kintyre' won many awards for Wings. I went to one ceremony in Oxford Street at which Paul collected about six gold discs, as writer, artist, producer and boom, boom, boom. He needed gold discs like I need a bacon sandwich but I was still very touched and proud when Paul and Linda gave me one of them. 'This is for all the hard work you put into making it a success,' they told me and it still hangs on my wall at home.

I heard another story about that occasion which Linda told me at the time and I never dared argue with her. It seems that when they got to their St John's Wood home after the ceremony, Linda asked Paul if the records were actually gold.

'I doubt it, it's just a record sprayed with gold paint,' replied Paul.

'Well, can you still play them?' asked Linda.

Paul decided to find out so he took one of the discs he'd just been awarded, put it on the record deck and what did they hear? Max Bygraves on one of his 'Sing-A-Long-A-Max' records. I've never attempted to play mine just in case it's Des O'Connor! Only joking, Des.

Chapter Eleven

another great star I was able to help during my time at EMI was Cilla Black, the girl who was discovered when she went to see The Beatles at The Cavern Club in Liverpool. By the time I met her Cilla had many hits to her name but she had also gone a couple of years without making a record. So when she recorded 'Baby We Can't Go Wrong' for EMI I went into full swing to get her back to the top of the charts.

One of the programmes I'd arranged for Cilla to appear on as part of the promotion was *Saturday Scene*, the London Weekend show presented by Sally James. Normally the show went out live on a Saturday morning but a week before we were due on I received a call from David Bell, the head of light entertainment at LWT. David, who had been the producer of the great Stanley Baxter series, was not the sort of man who usually rang people, he waited for them to call him, so I was surprised to hear from him.

'Eric, you've got Cilla Black on *Saturday Scene* next week,' he said.

'How do you know that?' I asked.

'Because I'm the boss around here,' he said. He then asked if I would call Cilla or her husband and manager, Bobby Willis, to ask if they'd mind recording the show on the Thursday instead of doing it on Saturday. I told him I didn't think it would be a problem and then he said: 'Tell Bobby I would like a chat with him and Cilla but I'm going away on Friday for two weeks.'

Cilla, Bobby and I turned up at the studio on Thursday and David Bell's secretary was waiting. 'He'll see you straight away,' she said. Bobby waited for me to join them but I told him, 'I'm only interested in the record, I don't need to be involved in your private business.'

So I chatted to Sally James while they held quite a long meeting. When they came out I could see they were both very excited and couldn't wait to tell me what they had discussed. LWT were working on some new shows including one called *Surprise, Surprise* and wanted Cilla to host it. I learnt later that David Bell had about five other stars already lined up to interview but when he saw Cilla's name on his *Saturday Scene* programme list he immediately knew she was the one he wanted.

Although I did my main job and got the record into the Top Forty I like to think that in a roundabout way I had done much more for Cilla by helping her into what would become a starring role for many years.

We've stayed friends ever since, as I have with all of the artists I worked with during that time, but I didn't realize just how much I meant to them until I actually left the company. Part of the reason I moved on was that I wasn't getting on too well with the head of EMI records, Bob Mercer.

Bob had worked for EMI for many years but on the less glamorous side of the business. He was an educated man with degrees in this, that and the other, and had a monster business brain. I, on the other hand, had only my street-wise diplomas but suddenly Bob could see I was the star of the show and not him. The joke going around the company was that my expenses had just gone platinum and Bob had heard the story of the Cliff Richard gold disc and the 'Eric-I'll-Send-A-Limo-Hall' nickname and decided to put a stop to it.

It seemed to me that he was trying to undermine my popularity by cutting back on my expenses but many of the stars started to complain. I remember Marc Bolan telling me that one of the acts he'd booked for his Granada show in Manchester, a band called Alfalfa, had been told they couldn't travel first class by rail with Marc and his group but were ordered by Mercer to go second class. Marc was furious and told me that if they had to go second class he'd go with them. It was all very petty considering the money EMI were making out of the records I was promoting so, when ATV offered me the job as Creative Director, I accepted. My new boss was to be Peter Phillips, whose father Jimmy had written that wonderful song 'Smile' with Charlie Chaplin. I knew he was not a man who would quibble about expenses.

I was pleased when his friend Jackie Gill rang soon before I was due to start working for them to invite me to dinner to meet a group I'd never heard of called The Goodies. But when I arrived none of the group was there, just Peter, Jackie and another ATV songwriter called Miki Antony. I asked where these Goodies were and I was told that we were meeting them at the Penthouse Club later. After the meal we went to the club and, as I climbed the stairs, I noticed all these bright lights and cameras everywhere but I paid no attention. Then I walked into the club and waiting for me was just about every pop star in London – so many I couldn't take them all in at first. When they started singing 'We'll meet again, don't know where, don't know when' I just burst into tears. It was one of the most memorable nights of my life.

Paul McCartney, Elton John, Cliff Richard, David Bowie, Rod Stewart, Freddie Mercury, Cilla Black, Blue Mink and even stars from rival record companies like the Bay City Rollers and Alvin Stardust were there. All the top DJs like Alan Freeman, David Hamilton, Kid Jensen, Noel Edmonds, Tony Blackburn and many more also showed up. David Cassidy and Shirley Jones, who played his mum in the TV series *The Partridge Family*, were in London and showed, along with many more showbiz people, making it a bash to remember. Even Bob Mercer, who I think by now had realized he'd made a big mistake in letting me go, turned up to wish me well.

I'll never forget one young lad coming to me and begging me not to leave EMI. 'Can't you wait a few weeks?' he pleaded. 'I'm about to have my first record released and I need you here to plug it.' He was Tom Robinson and the song was '2-4-6-8 Motorway'. Soon he went on stage to sing the song in a bid to make me stay but I told him he was wasting his time because I had no sense of direction. His performance led to everyone doing a turn including one of my oldest friends, Steve Harley of Cockney Rebel, who I'm delighted to see has had a revival recently. The party went on until the early hours but the memories of it will live with me for ever.

Chapter Twelve

my position at ATV Music combined all the aspects of the music business that I had previously experienced in my career. As Creative Director it was my job to put together a package by getting the work of the songwriters on the ATV books recorded and then to produce and promote the finished product. As the job title implied a bit of creativity was required to bring off this particular exercise and some of the ideas I came up with were not always appreciated by the artists.

One of the first I was involved with after my move from EMI was Elaine Paige. I had never heard of her until one of our writers, Brian Wade, mentioned her name as someone who had the sort of voice that would suit his music. Brian had Elaine under contract but when I tried a few of my usual contacts about making a record, no-one wanted to know. Then one day Brian rang and screamed down the phone, 'Elaine's got it, Elaine's got it.' I didn't know what he was talking about, what did she have, the measles, the mumps, what?

'She's got the lead in *Evita*,' explained Brian. 'It will make her a superstar.'

It seemed every female singer in the world wanted to play Evita but I hadn't heard of her either. Brian eventually came to my office and told me all about this lady from Argentina and about Andrew Lloyd Webber and Tim Rice and all the schtik about how Elaine Paige was now going to be a superstar.

It was during a meeting with Brian that Cliff Richard phoned. Brian was listening to my conversation which went something like 'Right Cliff, yes me, you and Bill Latham (that's Cliff's friend for many years) at such-and-such restaurant on Wednesday. Right Cliff, see you bubbelah.'

'Excuse me, Eric,' said Brian as I put the phone down, 'but I couldn't help overhearing, was that THE Cliff Richard?' 'Listen Brian, I replied, 'I know you haven't known me for long but in time you'll discover I only deal with "THE"s.' Very flash of me I know but that's how I was then. I've become much more modest in my old age.

Anyhow, back to Elaine and *Evita*. Brian told me that since she'd got the part every major company, including Lloyd Webber and Rice, was now trying to buy her contract from him and he wanted to know what he should do. 'Tell them all to eff off,' I told him. 'You've spent money on this young lady and now that she's cracked it, please God, we can get some of it back by doing an album with you as the producer.'

Brian agreed and I was soon organizing the package. One of my first calls was to my old EMI colleague Vic Lanza who was in charge of their middle-of-the-road productions, handling artists like Roger Whittaker and Vince Hill. When I told him I had Elaine Paige and wanted to do an album produced by Brian Wade, he wasn't too happy. Over the years he'd had many meetings with Brian, who was trying to sell songs or artists he represented, and they usually ended with the message from Vic 'Don't call us, we'll call you' which he never did.

Now Brian had a star everyone wanted, including Vic. 'Fine Eric, we'd love an album with Elaine but not produced by Brian,' he told me. I put on my best Yiddish accent and told him, "Don't be a schmuck, Vic. If you want Elaine Paige you take Brian and not only as producer but as the writer of the songs on the album.' I could hear Vic spluttering and trying to hide his anger but in the end he agreed and so it came about that the first album ever made by Elaine Paige was not from *Evita* but on the EMI label and every song on it was written and produced by Brian Wade.

I always remember doing a deal to get Elaine on *The Basil Brush Show* on the BBC. It was a very popular programme watched by the sort of people I thought might go for the type of music on the album. When I told Elaine she said, 'Basil who?' I explained what the show was and she looked at me as if I was mad and asked, 'Do you think I'm going on a show compered by a fox with someone's hand up its arse?' I could see the funny side of it but I have to admit Elaine and I never really hit it off.

I had even worse problems with another lady I decided to be creative with, the comedy actress Hylda Baker. I came up with the idea of putting her and Arthur Mullard together to do a version of the Olivia Newton-John and John Travolta hit 'You're The One That I Want'.

First of all I sold the idea to Peter Prince, the head of A & R at Pye Records. I did my impression of Arthur and Hylda singing the song down the phone and Peter laughed so much he agreed to make the record. I then got hold of singer Kenny Lynch, now one of our writers and a very good friend, and asked him if he'd produce the record with one of Tony Hiller's songs, 'Save Your Kisses For Me' as the B-side.

All I had to do then was persuade Hylda and Arthur to go for the idea. I had never met either of them but within four hours I'd contacted both and talked them into the idea of making a record without telling them exactly what it was.

We arranged a meeting with Peter Prince and his boss at Pye, Louis Benjamin, to sign the contract. Before that meeting I called

Kenny, Hylda and Arthur to my office to explain what the record was all about. 'It's to be a send-up of "You're The One That I Want" from the film *Grease* but all you've got to do to make it funny is just sing it in your own voices,' I said. 'I like that song,' said the lovely Arthur. 'They're always playing it on the jukebox in my boozer.' When I mentioned the money involved all he said was: 'As long as I can earn enough for a pint and a cheese roll I'm happy.'

But Hylda's reaction was very different. Firstly she said she'd never heard of the song and wanted to know why she couldn't record one that she'd written. Then she went on the attack against Arthur. 'I'm an actress, you know. I've worked with Rex Harrison and Laurence Olivier but I can't work with this man. Listen to the way he talks, he's so common,' she said. I explained that Arthur was very famous for his television roles only for her to reply, 'I know, but he's not an actor, is he? Why can't I make this record on my own?'

Having convinced her that it's difficult for one person to sing a duet I finally got her to come to the Pye office in Great Cumberland Street. When Hylda arrived she forgot all about the record and started hustling Louis Benjamin who, as head of Moss Empire, organized the Royal Command Performance every year along with Val Parnell, Lord Delfont and my overall boss Lew Grade. 'Louis, why haven't I been on the Royal show for so many years?' she kept asking. In the end we got the contract signed and the record made and it was a monster hit here and all over Europe, and became a number one in Australia. It even got into the Top Seventy-five in America which was amazing because Hylda and Arthur were completely unknown over there.

There were many more tantrums to come from Hylda while we were promoting the record. She was a great lady when in the right mood but absolutely impossible to please at other times. On one occasion we were pushing the record by doing a series of interviews with local radio stations. One of them was Radio Aire in Leeds and the trouble started when we got into the limousine I'd hired to take us to Yorkshire. When Arthur Mullard tried to join Hylda, Kenny and myself in the back of the limo she said: 'You can't sit here you know, you're only a second-rate artist, you get in the front with the driver.' Arthur replied, 'I don't want to sit with you anyhow, you old cow'. Kenny and I both told him to take no notice and to join us in the back. 'No, f*** her, I'll sit in the f******* front,' he said, and that's emmes.

So we didn't have the best journey ever but eventually we arrived at Radio Aire where a lady was waiting to escort us into the studio. 'OK, bubbelah,' I said to Hilda, 'in we go.'

'I'm not going in there,' she said.

'Yes you are, Hylda, we're doing an interview remember.'

'I'm not doing nothing in there, have you seen that?'

'What, dear? Seen that what, where?'

'That there board up there.'

'Yes, it says Radio Aire welcomes Arthur Mullard, Hylda Baker, Kenny Lynch and Eric Hall.'

'I'm not appearing on no radio station what says that. I've been a star all over the world and I'm not taking second billing to no second-rater. It should say "Radio whatever it is welcomes Hylda Baker and Arthur Mullard".'

By now Kenny had had it with her and was threatening to knock her out while I did some fast talking to the radio people to get the message changed while at the same time apologizing to Arthur. 'I don't care, let her have what she wants, the silly old slag,' was all he said.

She was just as bad when we were making the video. Instead of doing it in a posh amusement park like they did in the Travolta film we took them to one of those real gypsy-type funfairs. They each had a little caravan as a changing room and one of the gypsy children wanted their autographs. She went to Arthur's caravan first and, as always, he said 'Certainly my dear,' and signed her piece of paper, 'To lovely Mary, love Arthur Mullard.' Then she went to Hylda's and knocked on the door. 'Can I have your autograph please?' she asked.

'Certainly my dear, what's your name?' replied Hylda.

She told her it was Mary and handed her the piece of paper and pen. Suddenly Hylda started hollering, 'I can't sign that. How dare you ask me?' Little Mary started crying and her mother turned up to ask what was wrong. 'She wants me to sign my name under his. I'm not doing that. I want my own piece of paper.' said Hilda. She then slammed the door in the child's face.

Hylda was even a nightmare when she and Arthur appeared on *Top Of The Pops*. It's well known that if you appear on that show the sales of the record go crazy for a week. But after watching her appearance I knew it was going to be the only time in history a record that was soaring up the charts would drop twenty places. Hylda could never remember the words so they put up what are known as idiot boards which contained all the lines from the song for her to read. But, as I soon discovered, it was a disaster as Hylda was always five or six words behind Arthur. Then she started waving to me at the side of the stage to tell me to get her glasses out of her handbag. She couldn't see the words, would you believe. I'd finally discovered why they call them idiot boards.

On another occasion I was in the White Elephant restaurant with Hylda when another fine actress, Liz Fraser, who was dining with friends, came over to our table to say hello. But Hylda was in one of her most hateful moods and did her prima donna bit. 'Who are you? I don't know you, do I?' she said to Liz in such a loud voice that everyone in the restaurant could hear what she was saying. Naturally, it was very embarrassing for Liz and she decided that drastic action was needed. She leant over and whispered in Hylda's ear, 'If you don't make a fuss of me I'll give you a kick in the crutch.'

Immediately Hylda leapt to her feet, gave Liz a monster kiss and shouted: 'Lovely to see you again darling.'

The most infuriating incident involving Hylda came when she appeared on Pete Murray's programme, *Open House*. There was a gimmick on the show in which Pete would ask his guest what their favourite song was and then surprise them by just happening to have the record at hand. In order to do this they needed to discover the song in advance without the guest knowing and I was asked to do this by the producer, Dennis Jones. But I told Hylda what was happening and said, 'Pete Murray will ask you what your favourite song is and you'll tell him, he'll put it on and like the good old pro you are you'll sound surprised that he has it. OK.'

She said it was so I asked her what her favourite song was. '"She Knows You Know",' she said.

'No, Hylda, you wrote that,' I replied. 'Someone else's song.'

'"Nearest And Dearest".'

Again I had to explain to her that Peter was going to play her songs anyhow. 'He wants a song by someone else that you like.'

'I don't like anyone else's songs, only my own,' she replied. After an eternity Hylda finally said that she liked a song called 'You Made Me Care' but added, 'You will never have heard of it though.' As it happened it was also a favourite of mine and I surprised Hylda by singing it to her over the phone: 'You made me care when I wasn't in love, now that I'm caring you're gone.'

She was still talking about how thrilled she was that I knew the song when I took her to the studio the following day. The interview went well until Pete got to the question. 'Tell me Hylda, do you have a favourite song?'

'No, I don't,' replied Hylda, which naturally threw him a bit.

'Are you sure?'

'Of course I am.'

Finally he was forced to say, 'A little bird told me "You Made Me

Care" was a favourite of yours.' 'Never heard of it,' snapped Hylda and that was that.

What a woman! Kenny Lynch said he would never work with her again following another bust-up when we were all having dinner in a restaurant called September in the Fulham Road. Arthur was a great movie buff and he asked Kenny who his favourite female stars were. 'The usual,' said Kenny, 'Bette Davis, Barbara Stanwyck, Doris Day, Judy Garland.'

'Excuse me, I'm very angry with you,' interjected Hylda.

'Why, we haven't had a row have we?'

'Haven't had a row! This man Mullard, who calls himself an actor but isn't, asked you who your favourite actresses were and you never mentioned me.' She stormed out and didn't speak to any of us for about three days.

When Louis Benjamin discovered that the record was such a success in Australia, he wanted to do a follow-up album and was offering good money but when I told Kenny about the offer he didn't want to know. 'I won't work with her again and neither will Arthur,' he said. When I told him how much it was worth he changed his mind but we still had the problem of getting Arthur to work with Hylda again. And I can reveal now, for the first time, that I did it by lying to both Hylda and Arthur. I told them both that they were doing solo albums. They both came into the studio at separate times and did their bit and we put the two tracks together to make the album. It was hilarious at times with me doing my James Bond bit by arranging with the driver of the car bringing Arthur to the studio to stop and phone us when he was a certain distance away to give us time to get Hylda out of the studio before he arrived. They never worked out what was happening and, not unsurprisingly, the album was a total flop.

Chapter Thirteen

my involvement with Kenny Lynch in the Hylda Baker saga was just one of many hilarious ventures we shared. It was odd that we should get together when I joined the Lew Grade organization because Kenny had been involved with the great Sir Lew for a long time.

He once told me of the night he was appearing in a show in Brighton when the lovely Alma Cogan topped the bill. At that time Lew Grade was probably the biggest showbiz agent of them all. He handled everybody who was anybody, anyone who was anyone and even anyone who was no-one. After the show Lew went backstage where he bumped into Kenny. He said, 'You were sensational, son. I don't want to knock your agent but you should have been much higher up the bill, who's handling you?'

'You are, Mr Grade,' answered Kenny.

Lew, of course, was the brother of Leslie Grade and Bernard Delfont, the organizers of the Royal Command Performance. One year when the Queen Mother was at the show she was introduced to the mother of the Grade boys.

'I must say,' said the Queen Mother, 'your family has done very well.'

'Thank you, Ma'am,' replied Mrs Grade, 'and may I say yours hasn't done too badly either.'

When I later became an agent I was asked, 'Are you any relation to Lew Grade, because you are Jewish, you smoke big cigars and like him you never stop talking?'

'No, I'm not related,' I answered. 'In fact, if he's Lew Grade I reckon you should call me Low Grade.'

Kenny will kill me when he reads this next story because I'm about to reveal a secret I've kept from him for many, many years. He and I had been in Paris to meet and work with the marvellous American star Ginger Rogers with whom I had done some promotion work. On this occasion she was doing a TV show to which Kenny and I were invited and she later took us to dinner. After we'd finished our meal Kenny and I went to the airport for our flight home and I took the baggage and the tickets and did the business at the check-in. Eventually the flight was called and so we went to the boarding gate.

'Boarding passes please,' said the man at the gate.

'I haven't got a boarding pass,' I told him. Kenny said, 'You must have them, Monster, they hand them out when you check in the luggage.'

'No, they never gave them to me,' I insisted.

Suddenly it all got a bit hairy. I was arguing that I never had them and Kenny was telling them: 'If Eric Hall says he hasn't been given the boarding passes then he hasn't.' He was threatening to fight them all, claiming they are anti-English, anti-black and anti-everything else he could think of.

The police were called but they wouldn't let us on the flight and so it left without us. They told us to wait while they sorted it and promised to get us on the next flight, but we sat there for hours and three more flights left for London minus Lynch and Hall. Eventually they sent for the British Ambassador, emmes, who didn't know me from Adam but immediately recognized Kenny. 'I saw Ginger Rogers last night, she was wonderful, and I saw you in the audience, Kenny. Yes, no problem I'll sort this.'

He then spoke to the authorities who decided we could leave on the next flight. Unfortunately that wasn't until the following morning so, rather than stay in the airport, we decided to go back to the hotel we'd stayed in the night before. It was the famous George V hotel and our bill for the previous night had been paid for by Ginger Rogers. When we arrived they made a fuss, saying, 'Ah, yes you were Miss Rogers' guests but I'm afraid she has already left.'

'Yes, I know but book us a couple of rooms and I'll pay,' I said cockily.

'Certainly sir, that will be ...' and he named a price which even by my platinum expense account standards was ludicrous. So we moved to the Holiday Inn. Next morning we got on the flight and with a sigh of relief returned to London with Kenny giving it a non-stop whinge about the French airports, French hotel prices and boom, boom, boom. He was ready to go to the newspapers, give them the story and declare war on France.

When we arrived at Heathrow I went to the toilet. I put my hand in my trouser pocket and what did I find? Yes, you've got it, the boarding passes. I must have looked everywhere except in that pocket. I didn't dare tell Kenny that I'd had them all the time because I'm sure he'd have lived up to his name and lynched me on the spot. And I've never told him since. Sorry Ken.

Another story involving Kenny concerns a record idea we had for that lovely comedian Larry Grayson who was an ATV star and was red hot at the time with his show *The Generation Game*. Kenny and I decided to take him for Sunday lunch to discuss the project but, typically of a Jewish organization, every one else had a company car but we had a company boat. 'Take Larry for a sail up the Thames and stop for dinner in that nice hotel at Maidenhead,' said Peter Phillips.

So off we went and after a short while Kenny, who was driving or whatever it is you do with boats, said: 'When we get to the locks, Monster, you do the business.'

'What do I have to do?' I asked.

'Well, you have to jump off and tie us up while the water rises.'

'Are you mad? The only locks I know about are bagels and lox.'

'I'll show you how to do the first one then you do the next,' said Kenny.

'No way. I'm Jewish and everyone knows Jews don't swim,' I argued.

Then in stepped Larry. 'Don't worry about it, my loves. I can't swim either but I'll do the locks.'

'Don't be silly,' I said, 'What happens if he falls in the water?'

'We'll throw him a buoy,' said Kenny.

And, quick as a flash, Larry said: 'If I fall in the water it would be no time for romance.'

Larry actually did make a record called *Shut That Door* but unfortunately it wasn't for us so perhaps the boat wasn't such a good idea after all.

Max Bygraves was another of my close friends in those ATV days even though he wasn't involved in our company. I'd known Max for many years and, like myself, he was proud of his London background. He once told me that his father worked for a Jewish tailor in the East End named Harry Levy and they worked a scam in which Max's dad pretended to be deaf.

There were no price tags on the suits in the window so whenever anyone asked how much a certain suit was Max's father would shout up the stairs: 'Mr Levy, how much is the blue pinstripe?'

'Thirty shillings,' Mr Levy would shout back, making sure the punter could hear him. 'How much?' Max's dad would yell, holding his hand to his ear.

'Thirty shillings.'

'Thirteen shillings,' Max's dad would tell the customer and

they'd buy two, thinking they'd made a profit when in fact the suits only cost ten bob each.

Max also told me a story about a visit he made to Ireland. His wife's birthday was coming up so he went into a large department store to buy her a gift. As soon as he walked in he was mobbed by everyone – customers, staff and management – all wanting his autograph. After signing for hours he finally made his purchase and offered a cheque as payment. 'Thank you Mr Bygraves,' said the assistant who had been clamouring for him minutes before, 'do you have any identification please?'

While I was at ATV I got a call from Max asking if I could meet him at the Embassy Club where he was making a video for his latest album, a sort of disco version of his *Sing-Along-A-Max* series. Although I wasn't involved he asked if I could help out so I went along. I gave him some advice he wanted and while I was there I discovered he'd been having a major problem with the promotions man for the company making the video. Max had asked them to get him white top hat and tails because it was summer time and he felt black wouldn't look right. 'I've been waiting six weeks and here we are ready to film and still they haven't got it for me,' moaned Max.

The promotions man said, 'I've tried everywhere and although I can get the suit I can't get a white top hat, all they've got is black or grey.'

'Why don't you get the black one and dye it white?' I suggested.

And Max looked at the poor schmuck and said 'See, that's why Eric is who he is and you are who you are.' I took that as a great compliment from a great performer.

Chapter Fourteen

althrough I've always hated flying I had to do it often in my job with ATV because of the monster contacts we had in America. I was able to overcome my flying phobia because I knew that every time I crossed the Atlantic I would meet more famous people and I was still very star-struck despite the many top celebrities I'd already worked with in England and America.

Of course, it's not the actual flying bit that I hate, it's the thought of crashing that scares me. And I'm happy to say that I once got a laugh from the great American comedian Jack Benny, who was notorious for keeping a straight face, when I told him that. He also told me a funny aeroplane story. He claimed that every time he got on a plane all the other passengers got off. I asked why and he explained: 'When I get on the plane someone always recognizes me and shouts "Hi Jack". Then everyone else on the plane thinks there's a terrorist on board and runs for the exit.'

I also once had an amazing flight from Nashville to New York with that fantastic character Dean Martin who was just as well known for his drinking as he was for his singing. I'm not saying he was drunk when we boarded the plane but he fell asleep as soon as he sat down. As we were taxi-ing to the runway, I looked out of the window and saw flames coming out of one of the engines. I immediately panicked, shook Dean awake and pointed to the flames. He just looked out of the window and said 'Funny place to hold a barbecue,' and immediately went back to sleep.

Most of the stars I was dealing with at that time were the very tops, among them were Frank Sinatra, Tony Bennett, Sammy Davis, Ginger Rogers, Jimmy Cagney. But my first success for ATV on the other side of the pond came with a singer I'd never heard of before arriving in America.

It started when I was travelling with Peter Phillips in a taxi from Kennedy Airport to our hotel in New York and heard a song on the cab driver's radio. I didn't recognize the voice but I was monster impressed with the lyrics and tune and asked the driver if he'd mind turning the sound up. 'Sure thing buddy, you like it huh?' he said, in that voice only New York cabbies seem to have.

I told him I thought it was a knock-out and asked who was singing. 'No idea buddy, it's a new one on me,' he said. Just then the record ended and the DJ said 'That's the latest release from Dan Hill and it's called "Sometimes When We Touch".' Neither Peter or I had heard of Dan Hill but I discovered the name of the radio station from the cab driver and then called it from the hotel to ask what label the record was on. As it happened Peter Phillips knew the owner of that particular company and contacted him to find out if Dan Hill had a deal with any record or publishing company in England.

He told us that he didn't and that although all the major labels had been offered the record they'd all passed on it. I couldn't believe my luck 'They're all mad,' I told Peter. "I'm absolutely certain this number will be a smash hit in England.' We immediately organized a meeting with both the record company and Dan Hill, who lived in Los Angeles, and within two days ATV owned the English publishing rights for that song and many more written by Hill.

I'm glad to say I was proved right. We got Pye to release the song as a single in February 1978 and it was such a monster success that Dan was invited to visit England to make an LP. I went to the airport to meet him when he arrived with his manager who, would you believe, was named Bernie Finklestein. 'Hello Bernie, are you Jewish?' I asked. 'Are you mad,' he replied, 'is the Pope a Catholic?' I asked if they had any luggage to collect and Dan, who was wearing one of those country and western-style shirts made up of multi-coloured patches, said, 'What do you mean luggage?'

'You know, suitcases with all your clothes in,' I replied.

'Nope, all I got is what I'm wearing,' he answered.

I immediately started to worry because I'd already arranged for him to appear on several television shows, including *Top Of The Pops*. Bernie could see I was puzzled and said 'Bubbelah, don't worry. We'll buy him some of that fancy London gear from Carnaby Street.' I didn't like to tell him that by this time Carnaby Street was a bit old fashioned but I figured if that's what he wanted I wasn't too worried. Whatever he bought had to be better than the shirt he was wearing.

Although it was getting late by the time we reached central London, Dan wanted to go to the ATV offices to run through a few numbers that he planned to use in the album.

My mate Kenny Lynch was with us and, being the nice guy he is, he started running around making sure Dan had everything he needed.

'I'd like the piano moved because the acoustics are not too good in this room,' said Dan and so Kenny and I pushed the piano into the next room. When we had finished Bernie took out a £1 note, gave it to Kenny and said, 'Thank you for your help, boy.' He sounded as if he was in Alabama or somewhere and obviously thought that because Kenny was coloured he had to be one of the porters. We had a good laugh about it later but I did point out to Kenny that he hadn't actually given him back the money.

Anyhow, a couple of days later Dan arrived at the BBC's White City studios for the *Top Of The Pops* programme. And, would you believe it, he turned up still wearing the same multi-coloured shirt which, I swear, he hadn't taken off since he arrived. Not only did it look worse than ever, it was now smelling pretty bad as well. His hair, which was long and greasy, plus the shaggy beard didn't do him any favours either. I have to say that although Dan was a lovely lad his personal cleanliness left a lot to be desired. I was wearing a very trendy cardigan which I'd bought in Take Six in Oxford Street that day and, in desperation, I gave it to Dan, saying, 'Wear that on the show, it will bring you luck,' not wishing to tell him that he looked like something the cat had dragged in. So I then had another claim to fame: Dan Hill wore my cardigan on *Top Of The Pops*.

The show went well and the next day we went to the famous Pye Records studio so that Dan could do some tracks for the album which was being produced by Bernie Finklestein. He was soon to prove that he did not have a clue what he was doing. I don't think he could have produced his birth certificate never mind an album.

The studio was what is known in the business as a twenty-four-track studio which means simply that you could make twenty-four separate recordings of instruments and vocals to make up one song. It was estimated that Dan would only need three or four that day but Bernie had other ideas. All we could hear was him saying to the engineer, 'No, I'm not too happy with the violins on that one, let's try it again,' or 'I think the background was a bit too loud that time, let's do another one'. Eventually the engineer said, 'That's it, Mr Finklestein, we've finished.' 'What do you mean finished, we've got it booked until midnight.' said Bernie.

'I know, but we've used up all the tracks,' explained the engineer.

'What's that room next door?' asked Bernie.

'That's another twenty-four-track studio,' replied the engineer.

'Anyone using it?'

'Not tonight.'

'Right,' said Bernie, producing a £20 note, 'nip in there and borrow a few tracks will you?'

He just didn't know what he was talking about which probably explains why the album was a total flop. But it didn't stop Dan Hill becoming the favourite singer of many people in this country, just on the strength of that one big hit.

Many, many years later I was in a London hotel with my old friend Jeremy Beadle when I spotted Eddie Levy, who I knew from my days as a record producer, and Bill Tarmey who plays Jack Duckworth in *Coronation Street*. Although by this time I was a football agent and out of the music business I was, and still am, a monster *Coronation Street* fan. So when I saw Eddie go to the toilet I followed him. We had a chat and then I asked if he would introduce me to Bill Tarmey. He agreed and when I got back to my table Bill joined us. 'Hello Monster, my son is always talking about you. He wants to be a footballer and have you as his agent,' he said.

I introduced him to Jeremy and we all got together for a drink. I hadn't noticed before but Bill and Eddie were with another guy who seemed a bit out of place, wearing jeans and sandals with no socks – a bit of a hippy. He looked vaguely familiar but I didn't really recognize him until Bill Tarmey said, 'Eric, do you know Dan Hill?' I couldn't believe it and suddenly Dan recognized me as well and we hugged each other and I said, 'By the way Dan, can I have my cardigan back now.'

It turned out that Bill, who has a very good crooner-type voice, was making an album and had asked Dan, who he admired so much, to write some numbers for him. And it turned out there was another fan in the room as well because as Dan and I were having our reunion Jeremy Beadle kept tapping me on the shoulder. 'Monster do me a favour and introduce me to Dan Hill, he's my favourite singer of all time,' he said. And, whenever we get together now, Jeremy always tells whoever we are with, 'Did you know it was Eric who introduced me to my idol Dan Hill?'

Chapter Fifteen

as you will no doubt have noticed by now, I do love to name drop but can you really blame me when I'm talking about greats like Frank Sinatra and Tony Bennett?

I spent a month with Tony when he was touring in England because I was promoting his latest single and organizing his TV and radio interviews. We were running late one day in Leeds and had to pack the cases and check out in a hurry to catch a plane to Glasgow.

'You check us out and I'll pack,' Tony said to me.

'No I'll pack you check out,' I insisted.

'Why?' asked Tony.

'Because you left your overcoat in Manchester, your pyjamas in Brighton, your tie in Newcastle and we all know what you left in San Francisco. So this time I pack.'

What a lovely man Tony is and while I was writing this book I met him again briefly when I went to the funeral of another dear friend, Benny Green, the jazz musician, writer and broadcaster. Benny had many friends all over the world but unlike me he very rarely talked about them so you can imagine my surprise when I arrived at Golders Green for the funeral to find Tony Bennett there. He had flown to London from New York and back again the same day just to be at the funeral. That's what I call very special.

Even more special to me was the day I met Frank Sinatra who I worshipped and whose death saddened me more than I can say. I will always be indebted to a man named Les Cocks for arranging that meeting with the great man. Les worked for Louis Benjamin, who owned Moss Empires and was one of the great impresarios like Lew Grade and Bernard Delfont, and one day he called to tell me that Frank Sinatra was in London.

'It's supposed to be a secret,' he told me, 'he's not doing any shows but is cutting some tracks at Pye studios. Would you like to meet him?'

Of course I wanted to meet him, so Les arranged for me to visit the studio during one of his recording sessions. I was aware that it's an American tradition when you meet someone famous for the first time to give them a little gift and as the day approached I started to panic. So I rang my pal Elton John who knew Sinatra well and asked what I should give him. 'He likes a drop of Jack Daniels, buy him a bottle of that,' said Elton. Although it's a popular drink in England now, in those days hardly anyone had heard of it, including me. I walked around London all day before finding a little shop in Soho that sold the drink.

When the big day arrived I sat in the control room with the sound engineer, clutching the bottle and looking through the glass panel down at Ol' Blue Eyes about two levels below us. There he was, wearing that famous hat and a pair of rimless glasses as he read the words of the songs.

There was I, Eric Hall, a little Jewish lad from London's East End, in the same studio as the greatest singer of all time. I just couldn't believe it was happening. Finally the session finished and Frank shouted into the microphone, 'Thank you everyone, that was great' and then he came up into the room where I and a few other people who had been invited to meet him were gathered.

I handed him the bottle and shook his hand. 'Thanks Eric, how did you know I drank Jack Daniels?' asked Sinatra.

'Elton John told me you might like it,' I stammered.

'You know Elton? Hey, he's a great guy,' said Frank.

It was now my turn to say something again but for probably the only time in my life I was speechless. Then I looked at the bottle which he had put on the table and I read 'Jack Daniels, Sippin' Whisky.' So I said to Frank, 'Tell me Mr Sinatra, why do they call it sippin' whisky?' He looked at me, took off his glasses and answered, 'Eric, you f***ing try drinking it.'

It wasn't the greatest conversation he'd ever had but I'm sure I'll never forget it. And, while I was with him, someone in the company recalled the story of the film he made with the rest of the so-called Rat Pack: Dean Martin, Sammy Davis Jnr and Peter Lawford, called *Ocean's Eleven*.

It seems that the producer sent Sinatra the script which was a story about a gang who perform the perfect crime by robbing a casino in Las Vegas. Some time later the clan met for dinner where Dean Martin said 'We all want to make the film, Frank, but it's no go without you. What do you think?'

'I think we should forget about the film and just do the robbery,' said Sinatra.

There are many critics who during Sinatra's life, and even after his death, tried to smear his name by saying he was involved with gangsters and the mafia and all that stuff. Well, I'm telling you now that the real Sinatra was not only the greatest singer ever, he was also one of the most generous men in show business. I know of countless people he helped of all religions and nationalities. He went to the rescue of many in the entertainment business who had fallen on hard times. When a fine actor named Lee J. Cobb was taken ill and couldn't pay his hospital bills Sinatra contacted the hospital and paid all the outstanding bills and arranged to cover any future expense, even though he hardly knew him.

Mind you, I did also hear a story which showed the harder side of Frank. His mother's favourite singer was not her famous son but a guy called Jimmy Roselli, who a few years back had a hit in England with a song called 'When Your Old Wedding Ring Was New'. One year when Frank's mother's birthday came around he decided he would ask Jimmy to attend the party, jump out of a huge cake, as they do in America, and sing 'Happy Birthday' to her. So he called Jimmy and explained that he was his mum's favourite singer and told him what he'd like him to do.

'Sorry Frank I can't do it,' said Jimmy.

'What's the problem?' asked Frank.

'I just don't do birthdays' Jimmy replied.

Roselli was a big favourite on the casino circuit in Las Vegas but, from that day on, he never played Vegas again.

Nevertheless, Sinatra was still a truly great star and I am not ashamed to admit that I broke down and cried when I heard of his death. Mind you, I still have tears of laughter when I recall another tale I heard about the time he was touring in England and had a gig in one of those big northern clubs where there was plenty of money to be made but the concert secretary was still king.

When Sinatra arrived for his rehearsal the secretary said, 'What will you be singing, Mr Sinatra?'

Frank started to rattle off his many hits. '"Night And Day"' he answered.

'Lovely number,' said the secretary, 'they'll all love that one.'

'"Come Fly With Me",' added Frank.

'Marvellous song, a big favourite of mine,' said the secretary. And so it went on until Frank said, 'And, as usual, I'll finish with "My Way".'

'Oh no, I'm sorry you can't sing that one,' said the secretary.

'Why not?' asked a shocked Frank.

'Because Charlie Higginbottom is also singing tonight and that's his song. He'll go barmy if I let anyone else sing it,' said the secretary.

The story reminds me of the night I took the great jazz pianist George Shearing to Terry Venables' club Scribes. George, who was blind, sat at the piano and started playing some of his great numbers like 'September In The Rain' and 'Lullaby Of Birdland'.

'I can't believe it, Monster,' said Terry. 'How did you persuade a great star like him to come and play here?'

'Ssh, he thinks he's at the Palladium,' I said.

Which is true-ish. I did take him to Scribes and he did play the piano and he is another charming man.

Sammy Davis was another man who I also had the honour of meeting once during my travels in America. I had often been asked how Sammy had lost his eye or if he had been born like that but he set the record straight for me when we talked. He told me he'd lost his eye in a car crash when he was a young man and for a long time he'd also lost his will to live. As he lay in hospital he had actually thought about committing suicide until a rabbi, who was visiting someone else, spoke to him.

He never told me what the rabbi said but he did say, 'It was after his visit that I knew I wanted to live and also that I wanted to take up the Jewish faith.'

I was reminded about that when I was watching a golf tournament on the television recently. Sammy was once invited to play in a celebrity golf event and was asked by the organizer if he had a handicap. 'I'm black, Jewish and I've only got one eye. Is that enough of a handicap?' answered Sammy.

He also told me that his mother was from Puerto Rico, which not many people know. 'I'm black and Jewish and she's Puerto Rican so when we move into a neighbourhood we clear everyone out,' he said with his usual laugh.

Sinatra, Martin and Davis. It seems hard to accept that three men who had such a great zest for life are now all dead. I feel privileged to have met them all.

Chapter Sixteen

t wo stars whose names will be remembered as long as movies and music exist are James Cagney and Ginger Rogers. Again I have no hesitation in shouting from the rooftops that I knew them both.

The wonderful Jimmy Cagney had originally retired from film-making in 1961 and after that turned down many offers to make a comeback. He was suffering from diabetes and, being a perfectionist, was worried that his failing memory would not allow him to learn his lines. But his doctor finally persuaded him that he would die if he just sat at home like a recluse and that he'd be better off working, so in 1981 he accepted a role in a film called *Ragtime* which was made at Pinewood Studios in London. That allowed yours truly the chance to fulfil another great ambition and meet the man I'd watched with awe when his great films were shown on television.

I was looking to do a follow-up record to the Hylda Baker/Arthur Mullard hit and Kenny Lynch and I had the idea of getting Jimmy Cagney to sing 'My Way'. Everyone in the world who thinks he can sing does 'My Way' but we thought that Cagney would be perfect for it. We could just imagine him singing, 'Regrets I've had a few, you dirty rat, but then again, hm, hm, too few to mention, you dirty rat.' So we put ourselves about and through the promotion people at the studio we arranged a meeting with Cagney. He turned up with his great friend and fellow actor Pat O'Brien, who played the priest in that marvellous film *Angels With Dirty Faces*. Cagney had insisted that O'Brien also had a part in this film although I suspect he really needed him for company and to help him when he had his memory lapses. I put the idea to Cagney and he said '"My Way", "My Way", I know that song don't I, Patsy?'

'Yes, it's Frankie's song,' said Pat.

'Oh no, Cedric (he never did get my name right once during the whole day), I won't do that song. I don't want to upset my good friend Frank.'

I tried to tell him that Sinatra wouldn't mind and that just about everyone else had recorded it at some time or other but he was insistent. I was amazed that the great Cagney, who had played the part of the hard man so often in films, was refusing to make the record because it might offend Frank who every time I saw him on stage would mime Cagney. But he remained adamant so we just had a pleasant lunch and a talk about the old days in the film business.

I asked him to explain something that had bothered me ever since I'd seen *Angels With Dirty Faces*. 'Tell me Jimmy,' I said, talking to him as if I was an old friend, 'When Pat as the priest in the film tells you that you have to act like a coward when you go to the electric chair, to stop all the kids thinking you were a hero, did the character actually act like a coward because of what the priest said or because he was really scared. The film never really explained it.'

'Well, Derrick,' he replied, 'I've been asked that question many times over the years. Did I or didn't I? Did I or didn't I? Did I or didn't I?'

Then he turned to O'Brien and said, 'Patsy, did I or didn't I what?' It was at that point that Kenny and I realized we'd got to Cagney a little too late and that a certain story we'd heard about him was true.

When we had first attempted to contact Jimmy we were told by one of the production staff that, as he had feared, the great actor was having trouble with his memory. So to help him they had designed a special pair of glasses which contained a hidden hearing aid through which he could listen to someone reading the script when he was doing one of his scenes as the chief of police. Everything went well until he was using a megaphone to talk to the robbers inside the bank. He said, 'You are surrounded you dirty rats, come out with your hands up. And George, if you've dropped off in the High Street can you pick up a Mrs Thompson outside Marks and Spencer.' He'd picked up a radio call from a local taxi firm and, like the monster professional he was, had just repeated it.

But he is still one of my all-time favourites and also a very modest man. I asked him during our meeting what were his favourite roles of the hundreds he'd played and he replied, 'Well Eddie, the best film I made was *Yankee Doodle Dandy* and the role I enjoyed most was a cameo part in the film *The Seven Little Foys* in which I did a tap-dance routine with Bob Hope.' So, despite all those gangster movies it was the musicals he liked most.

He also told me, 'I was just a hoofer who got lucky. There were better singers, dancers and actors than me about but I got the breaks,' and, as an egomaniac myself, I was humbled by his modesty.

I also had the pleasure of meeting that other great 'gangster', Edward G. Robinson, on one of my visits to America with Lew Grade in the early 80s. When he realized I was Jewish, he told me that he was also a Jew and that his real name was Emmanuel Goldberg. We went to a restaurant on Broadway and when we came out he said that, although he was now very old, he liked to walk instead of taking a cab so we strolled back to the hotel where we were both staying. After a few yards he suggested we cross to the other side of the street.

'Do you know why I did that?' he asked after a while. I admitted I had no idea. 'Well, on the other side we were in the shade and no-one could see my face. But this is the sunny side and you may have noticed that now everyone can see me and they're all saying "Hello" and "Nice to see you Mr Robinson" and that's important to me.' So now I do the same. I love markets because I can walk through them three or four times making sure everyone recognizes me. If it's good enough for Edward G. Robinson it's good enough for me.

And talking about egos, the lovely Ginger Rogers never failed to amaze me. I first met her when she was appearing at the Palladium and I arranged through her agent, Tito Burns, who I knew from the days when he was a musician, to meet her and discuss an idea I had for an album.

The meeting went well, she liked the idea and Kenny Lynch and I later took her out for dinner at the White Elephant restaurant on the Thames. We sat down and I looked around at the other guests and who should be a couple of tables away but Liberace. After a while he spotted Ginger and left the old gentleman he was with to come and join us. 'Ginger darling' he said and she replied 'Li, darling how wonderful' while Kenny and I sat there open-mouthed.

There was a three-piece band and a little dance floor there and soon Liberace said 'Can I have the pleasure of a dance Ginger?'

She accepted and there they were doing the light fantastic when I turned to Kenny and said, 'Isn't it marvellous Kenny, here we are a couple of East End boys watching Ginger Rogers dance with Liberace.'

Kenny replied, 'Which one's Ginger?'

We all had a good time and I even got to dance with Ginger which, as I said in the opening chapter, would have come as something of a surprise to the lads I grew up with in Bethnal Green.

We set up a date for Ginger to go to the studio to make the album which, strangely enough, was the first she'd ever made although she had sung many times in films. The only stipulation her manager had made was that there must be no cigarette smoke in the studio because Ginger hated the fumes. I didn't think there would be a problem but when I arrived the orchestra was already there. We'd planned for them to do the backing tracks and for Ginger to sing over them. As usual, some of the musicians were smoking pot and we had wacky baccy fumes everywhere. I was just about to start clearing the air when in walked Ginger who had arrived early.

She sniffed the air and asked 'What's that smell?' That's it, I thought, we've blown it. So, quick as a flash I told her it was the special air freshener we'd ordered for her.

'I love it. Get me ten cans to take back to America with me,' she said and I was left wondering where to buy canned cannabis.

Chapter Seventeen

after we had finished making the album with Ginger Rogers there were lots of kisses and hugs and thank yous and off she went, we thought, back to America. But a few days later I returned from lunch to be told by my secretary Louise, 'Ginger Rogers called and says she wants you and Kenny to have dinner with her next Friday.' Is she mad? I thought. How can we have dinner with her in America? An hour later Ginger rang back and said again, 'I've heard the album and I love it. Please have dinner with me on Friday.' I told her I didn't think we could get to America just for dinner and she replied, 'I didn't go to America, I'm in Paris doing some shopping and a couple of television shows. If you come over we can also promote the album.'

So Kenny and I flew to Paris and Ginger booked us into the famous George V Hotel for a couple of nights, as I related earlier. When we arrived, at lunchtime, I told Kenny I was starving and couldn't wait until dinner with Ginger before eating. I mentioned I loved the chips in France and Kenny said, 'I remember being here with Bruce Forsyth (he's a bigger name dropper than me) and we had a fantastic steak and chips. I'll take you there.'

Three hours later he was still trying to find it and I was exhausted, not just with hunger now but from doing a route march around Paris. Eventually he found the place and ordered steak and pomme frites twice.

'You schmuck, we've walked all this way and you still haven't ordered me chips,' I told him.

'Pomme frites are chips,' said Kenny. 'Everyone knows that.'

'Maybe everyone in France knows it but no-one in Bethnal Green does,' I replied.

Anyhow, we had the meal and then met up with Ginger. Later we all went for dinner in a beautiful fish restaurant opposite the Opera House where I dropped my second gastronomic clanger. 'Do you like bouillabaisse?' Ginger asked me. I thought she was talking about some sort of sport like baseball so I said, 'I don't know, I've never seen it played.' Kenny kicked me under the table and whispered, 'It's a fish stew.'

Ginger told us that she had heard her record on French radio and asked if it was on sale yet. Kenny remembered that there was a huge record store near the Arc De Triomphe that stayed open all night so we decided to take a look and it was then that I discovered just how devious Ginger could be and how big an ego she had.

There was a section in the shop called Easy Listening where all the middle-of-the-road music was on display. While I'm on the subject it's always amazed me why the big London record stores always put this type of music, which is the favourite of older people, on the second or third floor and there never seems to be a lift. By the time they've arrived on the right floor they've forgotten what they are looking for. But I suppose I shouldn't expect any better because recently I was in one of those stores looking for a Sophie Tucker record. An assistant asked if he could help me. 'Yes, I'm looking for Sophie Tucker,' I said. 'Just a minute sir,' he said, picking up the phone. I figured he was checking on the computer or something but then I heard him say 'Have we got a Sophie Tucker working for us?' Schmuck!

But back to Ginger. In the Paris store the easy listening section was huge and, I'm happy to say, was also on the ground floor. I asked the assistant where we could find the Ginger Rogers records and he immediately pointed out the correct section, although he didn't know it was Ginger Rogers with me. She wore dark glasses and a hood with a scarf over it and looked like something out of a spy movie. We started going through the albums in the section and found Fred Astaire, Astaire and Bing Crosby, Astaire and Gene Kelly, Astaire and Ginger Rogers in *Top Hat*, then a whole lot more of Fred Astaire on his own before Ginger finally found our record right at the back. She took it out and put it in the very front, which I would have done myself, but not content with that she then collected all the Fred Astaire records and hid them in the middle of completely different sections like Punk, Hard Rock and Country and Western, where no-one searching for one would ever possibly look.

Then she turned to Kenny and me, winked and said, 'Now let them try to find effing Astaire's records.' I was amazed to discover that despite the great films they'd made together, Ginger hated Fred. 'He always got top billing, it should have been Rogers and Astaire not the other way round – if only for the fact that ladies come first,' she told us.

Another great story I heard about Ginger concerned the actor Burt Kwouk, who played the part of Kato in the Pink Panther movies. It seems that when he was offered the chance to play that role in the first film of the series he was appearing at the Drury Lane Theatre in *Mame*, which starred Ginger Rogers. He realized that if the Pink Panther film was a success, which with Peter Sellers in the leading role there was every chance that it would be, there were sure to be follow-up films made and he was desperate not to miss out. However, his contract with the producers of *Mame* didn't allow him to leave for twelve months, unless they wanted him out. So his agent read the small print in the contract and told Burt, 'It says in this contract that no-one must smoke when they are near Miss Rogers, swear or say anything in her presence that might upset her. If they do they can be instantly dismissed.'

Burt saw his chance of being thrown out and went for it. He stood outside her dressing room with a big cigar, blew the smoke through the keyhole and said 'Go on you old slag, sack me. You can't act, you can't dance, you can't sing and you're an ugly old bitch,' and every other insult he could think of.

After five minutes she opened the door and asked who he was. 'I'm the Chinese waiter in the play,' said Burt.

'Why are you smoking that cigar?'

'What's it got to do with you, you old bag?'

'You're fired!' said Ginger. Burt had started to dance away with delight when she called him back and said, 'I'm feeling in a good mood today so you can stay but don't do it again.'

He couldn't believe his ears but, luckily for him, his agent finally did a deal with the producers that let him make the film and, as he'd predicted, it was a major success.

Chapter Eighteen

another lady I worked with on a record was the lovely Noelle
Gordon who was one of Britain's most popular soap stars at
one time as Meg Richardson in *Crossroads*.

As I was driving to work one day I heard on the radio that
Charles Denton, who had taken over as the head of ATV Television
which made the soap, had decided to cut the character out of
the programme and sack Noelle. It caused an outcry from all
her fans and I saw the chance of getting in on the act. I rang
her agent, a nice man called Michael Summerton. As you can
imagine he was inundated with calls but I finally got through and
told him I wanted Noelle to make a record and that I already had
exactly the right song. As usual, I was thinking on my feet but I
knew I could use two songwriters we had on the books called Tim
and Keith Attack who were former members of the pop group
Child. I'd had a song of theirs on my desk for about six months
called 'After All These Years' (a bit of a 'My Way' song but a nice
lyric) and I'd been waiting for exactly the right opportunity to
use it. Noelle Gordon's sacking was that opportunity. The song
was all about an actress who'd worked all her life on the stage but,

after all the years she'd given to her art, no-one wanted her any more. Perfect.

Mike Summerton loved the idea, the songwriters were delighted their material was being used at last, and I was confident I could persuade EMI to make the record. I sent a tape of the song to Mike Summerton's office for Noelle to hear and she was happy about it as well. Then Mike asked me, 'Can you have the record made and available for sale by Sunday?' Even though this was Monday it was still going to take some doing to get the musicians and the record studio booked at such short notice and have the record produced and distributed in six days. 'What's the rush?' I asked, and he explained that the story was going to be all over the front pages of the tabloids next day and the Meg Richardson Fan Club was planning a mass demonstration at ATV Studios in Birmingham on Sunday. 'There will be thousands and thousands of people there,' says Mike, 'so if you can get the record made in time and have them on sale in Birmingham you'll have a ready-made hit on your hands.'

It was the sort of talk I liked to hear so I went straight to EMI and put the proposition to them. They wanted to make the record but said there was no way they could have it available for sale in time for the demo. But they could provide a copy of the record which we could take to Birmingham and play over a loudspeaker system so the fans could hear it. We'd also be guaranteed plenty of air-time on all the radio shows and when the record did hit the shops in a week or so they'd all be queuing up to buy it.

All I had to do then was persuade Tony Hiller to produce the record. He agreed and on the Tuesday night we met Noelle, who was hiding from everyone at the Canary Wharf home of her good friend Clifford Davies, the showbiz writer. She signed the contract and agreed to be at the record studio the following day where we had the musicians lined-up to make the tracks.

Everything was going well until Noelle arrived. The orchestra had just finished doing their bit and were packing up to leave when she said, 'Eric, are all these people here just to play for me?'

'Yes, of course they are, Noelle.'

'Oh, isn't it wonderful. Not since I appeared in *Carousel*, *Oklahoma* and *Kiss Me Kate* have I had such a marvellous time. I must meet them all.'

'Well, I suppose there's time to say hello,' I told her.

A monster mistake! Noelle isn't satisfied with just an hello, it's got to be the full works. 'And what's your name? And what instrument to do you play? And have you been playing long? And did your mother encourage you as a child?' And boom, boom, boom forever. 'Bloody hell Eric, she thinks she's the Queen,' said Tony and I had to agree with him. She must have held us up for over an hour. We finally got her to sing the tracks and by working our proverbial cobblers off we got the disc made by Friday so we could take it up to Birmingham.

Noelle and I travelled up on the Saturday night to make sure we were there on time. We got to the studio early where the engineers had set up the speaker system for the record. I saw one of the station heads I know and he asked what I was there for. 'It's the demonstration for Noelle Gordon, they are expecting thousands,' I told him.

He rushed off to ask the police to turn out in case there was trouble and then we sat back and waited for the crowds to arrive. By midday nothing had happened and then, at about one o'clock, Mike Summerton phoned me.

'Has anyone arrived yet?' he asked.

'Yes, about eight.'

'What, eight thousand?'

'No, just eight.'

And that's all there were. They had a poster which read 'Bring back Meg' and they were all what we now call anoraks. They all talked like Benny out of *Crossroads*.

'Can I have your autograph Miss Gordon?'

'Certainly, what name is it?'

'To Syd, please.'

'Right to Sydney, love Noelle.'

'No, it's not Sydney, it's Syd.'

I have to tell you I've had some embarrassing moments in my life but this took some beating. And to make matters worse the record was a monster flop. There was a saying in the business that a record went into the charts like a bullet. Well, this one went in like an anchor, in fact only a major hype by EMI got it into the top hundred for one week and then it disappeared without trace. But it was a lovely song and could be done again. So if Barbara Knox, who plays Rita Fairclough, is reading this book and is about to get the sack from *Coronation Street*, get in touch, bubbelah, and maybe we can do some business.

Mentioning embarrassing moments reminds me of a meeting I had with another musical legend, Johnnie Ray, the deaf singer who took Britain by storm in the 1950s with records like 'Cry' and 'Walking My Baby Back Home'. He returned here in the late 1970s to do a tour and Tony Hiller and I came up with another idea for an ATV package. We decided to try and get Johnnie to make a record called 'Yesterday, Today And Tomorrow' which would consist of some of his old hits, some of the current hits and some new songs which would be written by Tony.

I contacted his agent and it was agreed we'd go to one of his shows and then meet him in his dressing room to discuss the project. The night arrived and Tony and I watched and thoroughly enjoyed the show. I know it's an old cliche that some singers get even better with age but with Johnnie Ray it was true.

When we arrived in the dressing room Johnny was drying his hair after taking a shower and was still in his dressing gown. As usual I couldn't wait and got straight into the spiel.

'Johnnie, you were monster sensational tonight and I'm now more convinced than ever that you are just right for this record we want to make. It's called "Yesterday, Today And Tomorrow" and it will contain yesterday's songs like the lovely "Cry" and "Walking My Baby Back Home", then some of today's hits like "It's Impossible" and "Feelings" and then some new songs that Tony here will write for you. Now I know you are due to go back to the States but your agent tells me you have no work lined up for three weeks so why not stay here. We've got the studio lined up, the musicians, the songs. We're ready to roll and all we need is the go ahead from you.'

I was talking nineteen to the dozen, I was sweating and after twenty-five minutes I finally stopped and waited for his answer. And he said, 'Pardon?'

I monster swear he hadn't heard one word I'd said because he'd taken his hearing aid out before having his shower. I turned to Tony and said, 'I can't go through all that again. Wait until he puts his hearing aid back on and you explain it.'

I'm glad to say he did, Johnnie accepted the offer and it turned out to be an excellent and profitable record which was re-released in 1998 on CD and still sounds as good as ever.

Chapter Nineteen

i have to tell just one more story about Tony Hiller. The monster hot 'Save Your Kisses For Me' made him a small fortune and one day while we were having lunch he said, 'I've decided to buy a Rolls Royce, come with me to help me choose it.'

We went to the famous Jack Barclay's showroom on the corner of Bruton Street but the salesman obviously wasn't too impressed with our appearance. He said 'Can I help you gentlemen' in the kind of voice which left us in no doubt he considered us anything but gentlemen.

'What do you think, Eric?' asked Tony.

'That greyish looking one is nice,' I said.

'That's champagne, not grey,' said the snooty salesman.

'How much is it?' asked Tony.

'£62,000.'

'I'll take it.'

The salesman was still not too sure about us.

'How would sir be paying?'

'I'll write a cheque,' said Tony.

'It won't bounce, will it?' he asked.

By now I reckoned Tony was ready to thump him. But he kept his temper, gave the salesman his bank's telephone number and told him to check. He did so, the bank confirmed it was all in order and now it was 'Would you like a coffee, gentlemen' and all that stuff but I did enjoy the ride home.

The story reminds me of Johnny Speight, another old friend who sadly died recently. He stood in for me on my LBC radio show when I was ill and I knew that he'd be playing a few Sinatra records because of what he told me when he bought a Rolls Royce after he had made it big with his Alf Garnett scripts.

He gave me a lift in his Rolls one day and asked if I had any new records coming out. It so happened I had a tape of a new group with me and I was about to put it into his cassette player when he said, 'Sorry Eric, you can't play it in this car.'

I asked why and he explained, 'Only Frank Sinatra tapes are allowed in this motor. This is a Rolls Royce and he's the Rolls Royce of singers. I'll give you a lift in my Mercedes next time and you can play your tape for me then.'

I believe that up until the day he died, which was not long after Sinatra, he kept to the rule that it was Frank and no-one else in the Rolls. What a great judge he was.

I know Johnny was no saint but he was a lot nicer than someone else I met who was supposed to be the Saint. Ian Ogilvy had taken the role over on the television series *The Saint* from Roger Moore. I knew a songwriter named Irving Martin who had written the new theme tune for the show, mainly because he was the nephew of Bob Baker who produced the series.

Irving was a lovely lad who had a monster stammer and one day he said, 'Eric, I've g-g-got this g-g-great idea. We'll do a r-r-record with Ian Ogilvy.' I had no idea what type of record he had in mind but, because of his connection with Bob Baker, a meeting was set up between Irving, myself and Ian Ogilvy in a restaurant called Rags, off

Curzon Street. I had never met the man before but I have to say I took an instant dislike to Ian Ogilvy as he always seemed to be looking down his nose at me.

'And where do you come from?' he asked.

'The East End of London.'

'Really, how interesting.'

Definitely not my sort of guy. He then added, 'I honestly don't know why I'm here. I only came because Bob told me to.' This didn't please me too well either.

'Well, Irving here thinks it would be a good idea if you made a record,' I explained.

'No chance.'

'Why not?'

'I can't sing.'

Irving was not going to give in that easily and he started stuttering and spluttering, 'B-b-but you don't n-n-need to sing these d-d-days. With all the t-t-techology we can m-m-make you s-s-sound like S-S-Sinatra.'

'I don't think so,' says Ogilvy dismissively. 'The nearest I came to a musical was when I was in drama school and they taught us to tap dance as part of the training.'

'That's it,' yelled Irving in triumph, 'we'll m-m-make a t-t-tap dancing record.'

In the end I had to put an end to his enthusiasm with the oldest joke in the book.

'We can't do a tap-dancing record, Irving.'

'Why not?'

'Because he'd keep falling down the sink.'

Chapter Twenty

britt Ekland, the beautiful actress who counts Rod Stewart and the late Peter Sellers among the men in her life, was also once engaged to another very eligible bachelor – me! Well, that's what it said in the American newspapers one morning and they are never wrong are they?

But, on this occasion they couldn't be blamed for printing what proved to be wrong information because it was Britt who had given it to them. I had met the lovely lady some years earlier in London but she had since moved to Los Angeles. I arrived there with Lew Grade for the premier of The Beatles' film, *Sergeant Pepper's Lonely Hearts Club Band*, to which ATV had the publishing rights. The day before the preview Lew suggested I find someone to take with me. 'You are our creative director and everyone turns up with a lady on their arm at these functions,' he told me. 'Fine, I'll ring Britt and see if she's free,' I said, and I was delighted to discover she was able to make it. You've seen what it's like at these posh affairs, all the stars make grand entrances, the cameras pop and the gossip writers ask daft questions. I wasn't even well known in England at that time, never mind America, so when Britt and I got out of our limo they all shouted, 'Who's your new escort Britt?' And she replied in that sexy voice of hers, 'He's Eric Hall, my music publisher, and I have to tell you we've just got engaged.' I couldn't believe my ears. 'Why have you told them that?' I asked as we went into the theatre. 'Because I haven't had my picture on the front page for ages and they need a good story to put it there,' she answered without a moment's thought. She'd obviously thought about it and had it all well planned.

We had a great evening and, as a movie buff, I was in my element at the party after the film at the Los Angeles Hilton where I met stars like Tony Curtis and George Burns.

Sure enough, next morning our picture was on the front page of the *LA Times* with the headline 'Britt To Wed Her Music Man'. Lew Grade heard the news and he called me to say, 'Eric, I know you are good at your job but you've taken it a bit too far this time. All I told you to do was escort a lady to the premiere, not marry her.' I naturally had to deny it the next day but that didn't matter to Britt, she was back in the news again.

My next meeting with Britt was far less glamorous. It was on a Christmas Eve when she was back in London and she asked me to take her to Heathrow to meet her daughter Victoria Sellers, who was flying in from America. After collecting Victoria I drove them to her house in Chelsea and she then asked if I'd join her for midnight mass at the local Catholic church.

'I can't go in there, I'm Jewish,' I told her, but she said it didn't matter what my religion was, I'd still be welcome. As I walked up the steps of the church with Britt I slipped and gashed my shin. There was claret everywhere and Britt and Victoria panicked. Luckily a priest saw what had happened and took me to a room at the back of the church where there was antiseptic cream and bandages. He cleaned the cut and sorted me out and I rejoined Britt and Victoria for the service.

The following day, which was Christmas Day, I rang my lovely mum Eva to tell her what had happened and she told me that as the priest was so kind and because it was Christmas, I ought to make a thank-you donation to the church. So I drove back there and asked the priest if they need a contribution for anything.

'Well, we do need a urinal,' he said, so I bunged him £100. When I got home I called my mum to tell her what had happened.

'What did you say they needed the money was for?' she asked.

'A urinal,' I replied.

'What's that?' she asked.

'How do I know? I'm not a Catholic,' I told her.

While on the subject of religion I'm reminded of the time I was desperate to get a message to Mickey Duff, the boxing promoter. I called his home and was told he was at the Marble Arch synagogue celebrating Yom Kippur. So I dashed over there and tried to get into the synagogue but I was stopped at the door.

'Excuse me sir, are you a member?' I was asked.

'What do you mean, it's a synagogue, not a club.'

'I know sir, but it is Yom Kippur. It's the busiest day of the year and we have to restrict entry to our regular worshippers who have been issued with a special ticket. If you haven't got a ticket you can't get in.'

'But it's urgent,' I said.

'No way sir,' he said.

I then explained that I would only be a minute and wouldn't need a seat. I asked him to just point out where Mickey was.

'OK, I'll let you in on one condition,' he said.

'Anything, what is it?'

'Don't let me catch you praying.'

That story leads me to another friend, the agent Michael Black, who had an office above a famous Jewish restaurant in Soho. He had an arrangement whereby he could order food by banging on the floor – two knocks would be a salt beef sandwich, three would be chicken soup and so on. Michael provided a lot of artists for shows on American Airforce bases in England and he often held auditions in his office for artists he might be able to place. During one such audition a whole array of food started arriving from the restaurant. Soon the office was filled with sandwiches, soup, coffee, bagels and boom, boom, boom. Michael suddenly realized what had happened and shouted to his secretary, 'Make sure we never have a Spanish flamenco dancer up here again.'

Michael is the brother of Don Black, the famous songwriter to whom I once said, at a time when I had a weekly column in the *Sunday People* newspaper, 'Comedy is in my blood, you know, Don,' and he replied, 'It's a pity there isn't any of it in your column, Eric.' I threw that one in just to show I can take stick as well as dish it out.

Another monster songwriting friend of mine is Barry Mason. He once told me about a journey he took on a train when he heard a man whistling that Tom Jones hit 'Delilah'. He couldn't resist leaning over to say, 'I wrote that, you know.'

'No you didn't,' said the whistler.

'I did, honestly. I'm Barry Mason and I'll bet you £10,' he said, figuring there was no way he could lose.

'Les Reed wrote it,' said the man.

'Ah yes, Les wrote the tune, but I wrote the lyrics.'

'Wasn't whistling the lyrics was I?'

I once met Ira Gershwin, who with his brother George made up one of the greatest songwriting teams of all time. Ira wrote the lyrics and George the music so I asked the great man which comes first, the music or lyrics. 'My boy, the contract always comes first,' was his reply.

Just to finish the songwriting theme, I must tell the story about one of my singer/songwriters at EMI named Scott English. He wrote a song called 'Brandy' which was a lovely song with nice lyrics about his dog but despite my best efforts, it only became a minor hit. Everyone forgot about it until out of the blue I received a call from the then up-and-coming star Barry Manilow who was touring England.

'I heard the record and I just love the song and want to record it,' said Barry. 'But I can't sing about a dog called Brandy. Can I change it to a girl called Mandy?'

I asked Scott and he said, 'He can call it Mandy, Dandy, Sandy, Candy or even Randy as long as he records it.'

Manilow stuck to Mandy and Scott made a fortune from what became a monster hit.

Chapter Twenty-one

I'd had a very successful time with ATV and was still enjoying myself when my old mate Elton John moved into my life again. In 1982 he stunned me by making a job offer I couldn't refuse.

By this time Elton was not just a great performer but also owned Rocket Records and the Big Pig Music Publishing company. They were doing all right, thanks to Elton's output, but were not having much success breaking other performers. Elton knew what I had been doing at ATV and wanted me to do the same for his companies. Although I knew I was one of the best in the business and was perfectly happy with my current position I was still staggered and flattered by his offer.

'How much are ATV paying you?' he asked. I told him the figure.

'I'll pay you three times as much. What sort of car have you got?'

'A Granada,' I replied.

'You can have a Daimler, Jaguar or even a Rolls if you join me,' he said.

'How much is your expense account?'

Again I told him. 'I'll treble that as well,' he said.

It sounded too good to be true so I accepted but I was soon to discover a few hidden snags and also some internal jealousies that would ensure I didn't stay with Elton for too long. But it was an exciting prospect to be back with the man I'd started work with in Denmark Street when we were lads all those years ago.

I discovered that Elton had nicknames for everyone, and they were all women's names. His own nickname was Sharon, after the actress Sharon John. His manager John Reid was called Beryl (Beryl Reid), Rod Stewart was Phyllis (never worked that one out), Freddie Mercury was Melina (Melina Mercouri), Prince Edward was Barbara (Barbara Windsor) and I was privileged enough to have two nick-names and sometimes three. My first nickname was Sophie which Elton explained was after Sophie Tucker. 'She had a big hit with "My Yiddisha Mamma" and that's what you are to me,' said Elton. But sometimes he called me Annie (after the film *Annie Hall*) and later Sophie got an addition to it following a dinner in London in which Cliff Richard, Elton and myself were joined by a few other friends.

Although I was now with all these famous people I was still an East End lad. As they say, you can take the boy out of the East End but you can't take the East End out of the boy. You'll remember my gastronomic gaffes from previous episodes and there was another one coming up in this restaurant. The menu was in French and I didn't have a clue what it said. But I'd heard Cliff say to his friend Bill Latham, 'Oh good, they've got fennel.'

What do I know from fennel? So when the waiter asked me what I wanted I said 'Fennel please.'

The waiter realized I was a schmuck and tried to do me a favour. 'And what would you like with it, sir?'

'Just fennel,' I told him, 'and make it medium rare.'

By now everyone knew I was out of my depth and watched with amusement as this green stuff was served up. It looked and tasted horrible but I had to eat it and from then on I had a new name – Sophie Fennel.

Elton switched the names around depending on whether he was happy with me or annoyed. Part of my job was to get other artists to record songs written by Elton – the same sort of deal I used to do with the ATV songwriters. One day I managed to get Frank Sinatra to record Elton's hit 'Sorry Seems To Be The Hardest Word' and when I gave him that news it was 'Well done Sophie, that's wonderful.' On another occasion I called to tell him 'I've got a whole album of your songs being recorded for Celebrity Records.'

'Marvellous, Sophie, who's making it?'

'Bobby Crush,' I said, and there was an explosion down the phone.

'Bobby Crush! Annie, what are you trying to do to me. Get it stopped. I'm not having some poncy pianist ruining my songs.'

'I can't get it stopped. The deal is already done.'

'Then get Ruth to undo it.' (Ruth is his lawyer Geoff Ellis's nickname, after Ruth Ellis.)

I'd always been able to make Elton laugh so I tried to get out of trouble by saying, 'You'll love the title of the album. It's called "Bobby Crush Plays Elton John And Loses". But even that didn't get me from Annie back to Sophie again and the record production went ahead, much to Elton's disgust. Bobby Crush never knew what was going on behind the scenes so, after all these years, I have to tell you Bobby – Elton definitely did not have a crush on you.

I was also still looking for new talent for the company to promote as I had done previously when I pioneered the careers of Queen, Pilot, Wizzard, Steve Harley and all the others. I could never quite match those heights but I came up with some talented bands like The Lambrettas, who were a very talented mod rock group, Judy Tzuke and Blue, who had a successful record released in America.

But although I was working harder than ever I suddenly started getting the feeling that things were not what they should be and that the cause of the problem was Elton's manager John Reid. He was also a lovely man but, in my opinion, he didn't like working too hard. Their relationship was different to the one that existed in most performer–agent or performer–manager partnerships. For a start they were more than just good friends, if I can put it that way, and also instead of taking 20 per cent or so, as most other manager/agents do, Elton had decided from the start to give John Reid 50 per cent of all his earnings. So he was as rich as Elton, and maybe even richer because he had lots of other strings to his bow that Elton never got a penny from. Over a period of time John had become a man of leisure while Elton was still out there grafting. Until I arrived if Elton rang the office from whenever he was in the world he'd ask for John who was hardly ever there so he'd have to ring back later. But when I joined the company I was always there so, instead of ringing back, Elton would talk to me. Then it moved on to the situation where he wouldn't bother to ask for John anymore, he just asked for me and I'd fill him in on what was happening about new records, new groups, this, that and the other.

It meant that the only time Elton spoke to John was if I was away on business, and, in my opinion, although it's never been confirmed, I think John became jealous of me because he was pushed into second place. He started to plan my dismissal and one day it came over something so stupid I can't even remember what it was. But I'm convinced Elton had nothing to do with it because soon after I left he asked me to call in to see him and asked, 'Eric why did you leave us, you had authority to do just about anything you wanted?' When I told him, 'I didn't leave, I was sacked,' he went white, stuttered and stammered for a few minutes and then changed the subject completely. That's why I'm sure he knew nothing about what John Reid had been planning.

As I say, they were very close and had a strong relationship until they parted company just before I started writing this book. John had managed other stars like Cliff Richard, Queen and Neil Sedaka for brief periods but he was with Elton for a very, very long time. I was upset that it all ended the way it did because I loved both of them and never intended to get in the middle, as it were. It was just the nature of our attitude to work that forced Elton and I together and pushed John aside.

I believe John's bitterness towards me remained long after I parted company with Rocket Records. Again I have no hard evidence for this but over the years when BBC or ITV have put on shows with top stars like *An Audience With Bruce Forsyth* or whoever I've always had an invitation and often been involved in the show in some way. But when they did *An Audience With Elton John*, to which I figured I would have been an automatic choice for an invitation in view of our long association, I never received one. When I asked a very good source why this was so I was told that John Reid had seen my name on the original list and had insisted it was removed, which really saddened me.

I should mention there was one other reason which made me think Elton knew nothing about my sacking. When I left I was due a certain sum as compensation but he personally paid me three times more than that. It meant I could live comfortably for two or three years without worry and it gave me the chance to be my own boss. Instead of finding groups and making money for EMI, ATV or Rocket I could now do it for myself. And, in conjunction with a record producer and songwriter named Andy Hill, it was working well. Our first project was with a group called Bucks Fizz, who won the Eurovision Song Contest, and I also managed and promoted a lot of other up and coming stars.

Then one day I had another of those meetings which seem to have happened to me so often in my life. I had had no thoughts about making any changes in my career until I bumped into Steve Perryman, the Tottenham Hotspur footballer. Before I knew it I was zooming off in a completely new direction and into a whole new world filled with very different people to those I had worked with since I left school.

Chapter
Twenty-two

althpough I can say, modestly as usual, that I'm probably one of the best-known football agents in England, I have never claimed to know anything about the game itself. In fact, my interest (or rather the lack of it) in football can be summed up by my answer to the question most fans ask each other: 'Where were you when England won the World Cup in 1966?' I know exactly where I was and it has nothing do with England scoring. I remember it because I would have been scoring with a young lady but for that final.

I vividly remember waiting in Debden for a 20A bus to take me home so I could get ready for a date with a lovely girl I had only recently met. The bus was there but there was no sign of the driver or conductor. After waiting for twenty minutes I went looking for them and eventually found them amongst a crowd of people gathered outside the TV shop window watching the match. When I asked when the bus was leaving they told me they were waiting for the game to finish. 'In that case I'm reporting you,' I told them. They gave me the sort of look that could kill then grudgingly returned to the bus. As we were pulling away, a huge roar went up from the crowd at the shop window. I realized later it was the moment Geoff

Hurst (now Sir Geoff, of course) scored his third goal and Kenneth Wolstenholme came up with his famous 'they think it's all over' line. It was certainly all over for me with that young lady because I was late for the date and she hadn't waited.

I tell the story to prove that my switch from the world of records to the world of football was about as unlikely as my rabbi eating a bacon bagel. But it happened because of a chance meeting I had with Steve Perryman, who was then Tottenham's captain. The chain of events which led to this monster change in my life started when I called at Morton's restaurant in Berkeley Square for a meal after returning from doing a show with Granada Television in Manchester.

Who should be in there but Terry Venables, who I'd met all those years ago in Denmark Street. We had a chat and he said, 'Do me a favour, bubbelah (yes, he speaks the lingo as well) come with me to Epping Forest Country Club.' I told him I'd had a long day and was tired but he said it was a charity event and they needed a few faces there. He also promised me a lift home. So I went and discovered it was being organized by the Tottenham players and when we arrived Terry introduced me to Steve Perryman.

I was standing at the bar when two other Tottenham players, Garth Crooks and Chris Hughton, introduced themselves. 'I know your face,' said Garth. 'Which football club are you with?' I told him I wasn't with any club and that I was in the music business.

'Are you a pop singer?' asked Garth.

'No, but I know plenty of them.'

Then he remembered he had seen me in Maunkberry's Club with Cliff Richard and Freddie Mercury and he started giving me a real ear-bashing about the stars I knew. In the end Steve came over to rescue me. 'Sod off and sell some raffle tickets' he told Garth who, being a smashing lad, did so without a murmur. Then Steve and I had a long chat and we got on very well because I made him laugh.

CHAPTER TWENTY-TWO

'Have you ever thought about being a football agent?' he asked.

'Are you mad?' I said. 'I don't know anything about football and besides I'm Jewish.

'What's that got to do with it?'

'Well you have all these free kicks in football, don't you? I can't get involved in anything that's for free.'

He told me I didn't need to know anything about football but I could use my showbiz know-how to organize commercial deals and he forecast, quite correctly, that football would become a monster sport commercially in the not too distant future. But I still wasn't interested and when he asked me if I wanted his number I actually said, 'No, but you can take mine if you like,' which sounds a bit arrogant now but I didn't mean any offence at the time, it just underlined my lack of interest.

If I really want someone's telephone number I don't mess about. I take their number, their mother's, sister's, brother's, friends', neighbours' – any number just to make sure I can get them when I need to. But with Steve I wasn't too bothered and it came as a surprise when he called a week or so later.

'It's Steve Perryman, remember me?' he asked.

It took time but eventually the penny dropped. 'Right, Tottenham,' I said.

'I'm coming into town this week. Can we meet?' he asked.

'Yes, where?'

'Do you know Morton's?' That was a monster coincidence because that was where I'd met Terry Venables before meeting Steve for the first time.

I turned up and he was with Glenn Hoddle, who I didn't like then and still don't now. He wasn't too keen on me either but we're entitled to our opinions about each other.

As a result of our chat I decided to give it a go as Steve's agent. Nothing to lose if it doesn't work I thought. 'We won't have a contract,' I told him. 'We'll just trust each other' and that's been the same with every player I've looked after ever since.

I didn't envisage then that I'd be involved in negotiating players' contracts with the clubs, I was just thinking of outside commercial deals. The first one I did for Steve concerned an idea I had for a programme on Radio Luxembourg which was still a top commercial station at that time. The idea was for Steve to host a programme in which a guest talked about a certain sporting year and all the top records for that year were played on the show. The first guest was Bobby Moore and the year, of course, was 1966. I also got Braun Electrics to sponsor the programme and for a twelve-week series I got Steve £50,000, which was a lot of money fifteen years ago. He couldn't believe I'd done it.

My next idea was to get a book deal for Steve. Now everyone does one, including me, but there were not too many around in those days. I also came up with the title, which I'm quite proud of, *A Man For All Seasons*, because he'd played so many seasons for Tottenham. So we were off and running with both of us enjoying the experience.

I still hadn't given up my record interests on the strength of a couple of deals with one player, but the word was beginning to spread and I next got a call from Alan Mullery, the former England and Spurs player. I didn't know who he was at the time but he told me he was a friend of Steve Perryman and also of a man named Don Walsh.

'Who does he play for?' I asked.

'No, you smock,' he meant schmuck but he was new at it, 'he doesn't play, it's his son Paul, who plays for Luton.'

Alan told me that Paul was about to sign for top club Liverpool but didn't have an agent. 'Steve has told us all about you and if you are good enough for him then Paul's dad reckons you'll do for him.' So we met and again I agreed to become his agent but again with no contract. Don Walsh couldn't understand why I didn't have contracts and I explained that it didn't matter if we had a ninety-seven-page contract, if Paul decided the next day he didn't want me as his agent then that was it. 'If he doesn't want me I don't want him and that's it. All the contracts in the world wouldn't change that,' I told him.

I offered him the same deal I had with Steve which was that I took 20 per cent of all the commercial deals I set up for him and his wages didn't enter into it, unlike other agents who were taking 20 per cent of everything. Both the Walshes were happy so we shook hands and I was on the verge of my first transfer deal in the cut-throat football business.

Chapter Twenty-three

In the spring of 1984 I travelled with Paul to Liverpool's ground, Anfield, where we met the manager Joe Fagan, the chairman David Moores and the secretary, Peter Robinson. 'Well, what wage do you want for this player?' Moores asked me. He was a lovely man really but it was still the days when agents were not considered to be respectable people and he was looking down his nose at me-ish. 'You've just paid £800,000 for him, you tell me?' I said, mainly because I didn't have a clue what to ask for. In the end they came up with a figure and I immediately trebled it. Paul was having kittens. 'What are you doing? I want to join this club, don't ruin the deal,' he said. He was so desperate to sign I think he would have paid them but he soon changed his mind when they agreed to my figure.

I was reminded of that story many years later when I was involved in the transfer of a player called Duncan Shearer from Swindon to Blackburn. I wasn't even his agent but when Kenny Dalglish, the Blackburn manager, rang to ask if Shearer was one of my boys I didn't say yes or no I just asked 'Why?' This was a trick I'd picked up in show business.

'Because we want to buy him,' he said.

'I don't think Southampton are ready to sell are they?' I asked.

'Not Alan Shearer you schmuck (he got it right), Duncan Shearer at Swindon.'

As it happened I had one or two Swindon players on my books, including Paul Bodin, so I asked him to get me Shearer's telephone number. I called and discovered he didn't have an agent. 'You have now,' I told him, 'and I've already got you a transfer.' When I told him it was Blackburn he didn't believe me. 'That's Kenny Dalglish, my hero,' he said. 'I've got pictures of him all over my bedroom wall.'

As with Walsh, when we got to Blackburn to discuss wages with chairman Jack Walker and Dalglish, I again trebled their offer and Shearer almost died of shock. He was so desperate to join his hero he'd have taken anything. But I triumphed again because I suspected I knew what they were up to. Swindon were their biggest promotion rivals and Shearer was scoring all their goals. I reckon Kenny didn't really need Shearer but he wanted to try and put Swindon out of the race and I think my theory was proved right because Shearer only played a few times for Blackburn and then they sold him to Aberdeen. Blackburn got their promotion but so did Swindon so everyone was happy with the deal in the end.

The fact that I was able to work that one out shows that I'd learned something about the game by then but back when I was doing the Walsh deal I was still very green about the way I could profit from a transfer and it took one of football's top men to show me the way.

I was adding to my stable of players very quickly now and one them was another Tottenham star, the Welsh international Mark Bowen, who was wanted by Norwich City. We arranged to meet their chairman Robert Chase, who was also one of the top men with the Football Association, at the Royal Lancaster hotel which is just around the corner from the FA headquarters. Compared to many deals I have done since it was plain sailing. We agreed the wages, the bonuses, the testimonial payments, the lot without a problem. It was an excellent deal for Mark and I was ready to leave when Robert Chase said, 'What about you Eric?'

'Pardon?'

'Well, we haven't discussed your fee. How much would you normally charge a player for doing a deal for him?'

I said that it was about £30,000 for a deal this big. 'Right, you put in an invoice charging us for, say, arranging our pre-season overseas tours next season and we'll pay you £30,000 plus VAT because I don't think the player should have to pay it,' he said. Clubs weren't meant to pay agents, you see.

I was eventually told to send an invoice for organizing a tour to Leningrad. I didn't even know where Leningrad was – I thought it was somewhere near Stoke Newington! But if you think that's crazy, another major Premiership club, I won't mention the name this time, paid me £25,000 for 'general scouting and public relations'. With my knowledge of football, I'd have more chance of finding Leningrad than new players!

Another time I was arranging the contract for David Howells at Tottenham. The chairman then was Irving Scholar and I swear every time I suggested a figure he increased it. I can't remember the actual amounts but let's say I suggested £15,000. He'd say, 'Tell you what, let's make it £25,000. No Eric, make it £30,000.' I couldn't believe my ears. He kept doubling everything I asked for. I was so excited I rushed out of the room and was just getting into the lift when his receptionist called after me, 'Mr Hall, wait a moment. Mr Scholar wants to see you again.'

'That's it,' I thought, 'he's sobered up now' and I half-thought about making a run for it but decided to go back. 'Eric, I'm so sorry but I forget to mention your fee. What do you think, £50,000?'

'Oh Irving, let's not be mean.'

'All right, make it £60,000.'

I'm out of the door like a flash again and, emmes, I'm just getting in the lift when she calls me again. 'Mr Hall, he wants you back.'

Is he taking the mick or what? Back I go and this time he says, 'Eric, I forgot all about the testimonial. I tell you what, we'll give him a guarantee of £150,000. In other words if he gets less than that we'll make it up. OK.'

Who needs agents when there are chairmen like that around? Mind you it was a bit different when I re-negotiated Howells' contract a few years later. By now Terry Venables was manager and he was doing the deals and although we were old mates he was much tougher than Scholar. After we'd agreed the wages and bonuses I waited for him to talk about my fee. Not a word. So I said to him, 'What about me then?'

'What about you, Eric?'

'You know, my fee for doing the deal.'

'I'm not sure about that. But if we can pay it how much do you want?'

Now David Howells had been sitting just behind me while I'd been negotiating. I turned to face him with my back to Terry so he couldn't see a thing. I gave David a monster wink and said, '£50,000.' 'Got something in your eye have you?' asked Terry. He may be a friend but, I tell you, I'm glad I didn't have to deal with him too often.

But I could deal with men like Scholar and Chase for ever and I was to be indebted to the Norwich chairman for teaching me another useful transfer market trick when I was trying to get Tim Sherwood a deal at Blackburn.

Chapter Twenty-four

When Kenny Dalglish was beginning to re-build the Blackburn team one of the first names on the list of players he wanted was Tim Sherwood of Norwich, who was also one of my players. In the light of my previous dealings with Robert Chase I felt my best bet would be to make a direct approach with the proposition. But Chase told me, 'I don't deal with transfers, Eric, that's all done by my manager David Stringer. However, if your player were to put in a written transfer request then David would have to consult me. And my advice might be that we should not keep a player who was unhappy with us and maybe we ought to sell. And I think he might just take my advice.'

What a good idea I thought and the next day Tim's transfer request was put in writing and within a week he was on his way to Blackburn. I have to say Robert Chase is probably the only man I know who would have made a better agent than I am. Well, ish.

But I've a few tricks of my own which might be considered a bit underhand. As far as I'm concerned, however, the only thing that matters is that I do the very best I can for my client. I remember when John Aldridge, then the star striker at Oxford, was wanted by

Liverpool to replace Ian Rush who they had sold to Italian club Juventus. Aldridge was my man and I knew it would be a monster move for him but Oxford was owned by Robert Maxwell who had big plans for the club and was not about to sell his best player. Maurice Evans was the Oxford manager and I was getting nowhere with him either so I came up with one of my clever little schemes to try and force the issue.

I contacted the sports editor of the *Sun* newspaper and when I said I had a big story for him he sent one of his top reporters to see me. Oxford were playing at QPR that night and before the match I met Aldridge and together we wrote out his transfer request. I then told the *Sun* reporter that it was being handed to Evans the following day.

Now, under normal circumstances that would not have worked, but I was banking on Maxwell's ego taking over. As he owned the Mirror Group I reckoned he'd be furious with Aldridge for leaking the story to a rival newspaper, furious enough to agree to the transfer. And just to make Evans angry I arranged for another reporter to say at the press conference after the match at QPR that he had seen the first edition of the *Sun* and it was carrying a story that Aldridge was asking for a transfer.

My ploy worked to perfection. Evans stormed in to see Maxwell who told him to 'get that f***ing Aldridge out of my club' and Liverpool got their man.

As I say, I have no qualms about pulling strokes like that when they are in the player's best interest and I have never been accused by any player of not giving him 100 per cent of my time and effort. In fact, I remember one player who reckoned I was making too much effort.

He was Johnny Byrne, a very good player who at the time was at QPR. I discovered he didn't have a boot deal so I arranged a meeting with a lovely man called Colin Wooldridge, the marketing manager for Adidas, and he agreed to give Johnny a contract. I met him at the training ground the following day and went through it with him. 'It's a three-year deal during which you have to wear their boots but you also get all their other gear free. And if they decide to drop you during the three years they have to pay up the contract in full. It's such-and-such amount per year but if you win the League you get so much extra, if you win any of the cups you also get extra and if you play for England you get a monster payment for each international. All right?'

Johnny looked at me and said very seriously, 'I'll never play for England.'

'Of course you will. I've seen you play and you're exactly what they are looking for,' I said, not knowing if he was or not but trying to gee him up.

'Sorry, Eric, but I'm telling you I will never play for England.'

I was getting really worked up now and told him, 'Johnny, that is no way to think. You have to be positive in this game, you have to believe in yourself.'

'No, it just won't ever happen.'

'Please, bubbelah, don't do this to me. I've worked hard for this deal. You can do it, you are a good-looking lad and if you just trust me you can be a superstar.'

'Eric let me tell you why I won't play for England,' he said. 'It's because I am Irish.'

Like I said, what did I know? He was already an Irish international but he didn't talk like an Irishman so I just assumed he was English. But, at least I'd done my best for him.

It was Johnny who told me of the phone call he received when he was with the Republic of Ireland team for a match in Italy. As usual he was sharing a hotel room with another player and when John answered the phone the operator asked for whoever the other player was. John passed the phone to him and heard him say, 'I know it is,' before putting down the phone.

'What was that all about?' asked John.

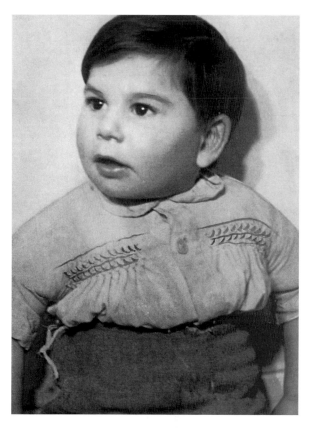

I've always said I look good for my age; here's me at twenty-four!

My lovely mother Eva holding me in her arms, with my brothers Terry (left), who passed away far too early, and Benny (right).

A day out with my father, Benny.

As a page boy at my uncle Tony Hiller's wedding.

Me (left) with my brother Alan and sister Caroline.

Partying with Jeff
Dexter, the sixties
DJ, Marc Bolan
and Bolan's wife,
Gloria Jones.

My brief stage career:
dressed as a frog at the
Wimbledon Theatre
with Marc Bolan.

MARC BOLAN

Marc gave me this
photograph of himself
shortly before his
untimely death.

A night on the town with my good mate Freddie Mercury
and his good mate Peter Straker.

Cliff Richard and his producer Bruce Welch present me with my very own gold disk.

With Britt Ekland on the night that she announced to the world that we were engaged!

A very special lady in my life, Barbara Windsor, celebrating her 60th birthday with (from left) Patsy Palmer, Lionel Bart, Scott Harvey, Danny la Rue, Dale Winton, Pam St Clement, Steve McFadden and me. I like to think I look good for my age but I have to say that Barbara looks better.

The night I introduced Jeremy Beadle to his hero, singer Dan Hill.
From left: Dan Hill, Coronation Street star Bill Tarmey, me and Jeremy Beadle.

Celebrating my birthday at Scribes with Tim Sherwood and Neil Ruddock, two of my football clients.

At the same party with Terry Venables and boxing promoter Mickey Duff.

And having a sing-song with my mother Eva and sister Caroline.

A bridal
'bung' for
Karren Brady.

With Dennis
Wise, who
always says
that I'm not
his agent,
I'm his mate.

'Some idiot told me it was a long distance from Ireland and I told him I knew that already,' said the player – who shall remain nameless.

Even I couldn't have organized anything better than the boot deal done by the legendary Stan Bowles back in the 1970s. When he got into the England team for a short spell he was approached by Puma to wear their boots at Wembley and he did the deal. He was then approached by Adidas to wear their boots and, being a bit of a gambler and always needing cash, he did a deal with them as well. So Stan now had the problem of trying to keep two companies happy in the same match. He got away with it by wearing an Adidas left boot and a Puma right boot. Now that's what I call pulling a stroke.

Another of my favourite football characters was also involved with QPR when I did their players' pool for the Milk Cup Final with Oxford in 1986. He's Jim Smith, who has managed more clubs than I've had salt beef sandwiches, but he was with QPR at the time and TV-AM wanted him and the Oxford manager, Maurice Evans, in a joint interview at 7 am on the morning of the Final.

Now, as all Jim's friends know, he likes a drink and is very funny when he's had a few. On this occasion he was staying in the Royal Lancaster Hotel and myself and a few friends were in the lounge bar on the night before the game. There was also a QPR punter there who had one of those glove puppets. This one was a monkey wearing a blue and white scarf and Jim took a fancy to it. He sat there with the puppet on his hand chattering away, saying things like, 'Who's going to win tomorrow then, monkey?' Then he'd pretend to be the monkey. 'QPR are going to win 3–0 of course,' and he went on like that all night. When I eventually left at about 2 am I said to Jim, 'Come on bubbelah, you've got to be up in a couple of hours to get to the studio. Time for bed.'

Jim refused to budge so I left him and went home to get a couple of hours' sleep. A car arrived at 5 am for me to go and collect Jim. I rang his room from reception but there was no answer so I asked the manager, who was a friend of mine, to give me a spare key. But Jim wasn't in the room. I eventually found him slumped in the same chair in the bar where I'd left him. I woke him up and asked if he wanted a shower or something before we left but he said he was fine so we went straight to the studios. I noticed he had a carrier bag with him but I didn't think anything about it.

Jim was in the London studio with the presenterswhile Maurice Evans was in Birmingham. Maurice looked very smart with his club suit, shirt and tie while Jim looked like a tramp in an old sweater and tracksuit. He sat on the sofa and the interview started.

'Are all your players fit, Jim?'

'I'll have to ask my assistant,' said Jim, and he dived into the carrier bag and came out with the monkey. I couldn't believe my eyes as he went into the act.

'Are all our players fit, mate?'

'Yes, all fit and we are going to win 3–0.'

He did that with every question. Maurice couldn't work out what was happening but, as usual, Jim got away with it.

I came across Jim again when he bought another of my players, Kenny Sansom of Arsenal, when he was manager of Newcastle. I went with Kenny to St James' Park to negotiate the contract and then returned to London leaving Kenny there. Newcastle were playing at QPR the next day and, because Kenny had left his boots at Highbury, I had to collect them and take them to the Kensington Hilton the next day where the team would arrive.

I saw Jim and explained that I'd brought the boots. 'That's all right, I'm not playing him in this match anyhow,' said Jim.

As I had agreed to meet Kenny in the bar I asked Jim if he'd join us but he declined. 'My doctor has told me that if I have one more Scotch it could kill me,' he explained. I met Kenny and had just ordered him a bottle of beer and a Perrier for myself when in walked Jim. 'I've changed my mind,' he said.

CHAPTER TWENTY-FOUR

'What would you like?' I asked. 'Perrier, Coca-Cola, Orange?'

'No, I'll have a large gin and tonic,' he said.

'But I thought you said the doctor had told you not to drink.'

'That was Scotch, he didn't say anything about gin,' replied Jim and that's been his philosophy ever since as far as I know.

Chapter
Twenty-five

One of the big jobs for an agent is running what is known as the players' pool when a team reaches a major cup final. He has to organize the selling of exclusive articles by players to the media, a pop record by the team and various other commercial activities. All the money goes into a pool and the players take an equal share.

One of the first I organized was the 1986 Milk Cup Final between QPR and Oxford, which I mentioned in the previous chapter. A couple of days before the match, Rangers had arranged an open day for the press at the training ground but, as certain players had already been bought up by various newspapers for exclusive articles, I wouldn't let those players talk to the rest of the media. I reckoned it would be unfair to those who had paid if the others got the same material for nothing. But one reporter refused to accept this and complained to Jim Smith, 'Who's the manager in this club, you or Eric Hall?'

'I am,' said Jim, 'why do you ask?'

'Because you have invited me here to meet the players but he won't let me talk to all of them.'

Jim, not wanting to upset anyone, called me over and said, 'Eric you little b*****d, why can't he talk to all the players?'

'Because his paper has not paid into the players' pool.'

'Well, that's not my problem. I'm fed up with the bloody players' pool, greedy bastards.'

'Yes it is your problem because you are in the pool,' I told him.

'Am I? How much is in it?'

'About £200,000 so far and if you win we could double that.'

'Then in that case,' said Jim turning to the reporter, 'in answer to your question, for today Eric is the manager.'

There was sequel to that story because the journalist concerned happened to be a friend of Jim Gregory, the QPR chairman and when the team lost the final he told him that they hadn't been trying because they'd already made so much money from the pool and that I'd worn them out running around and doing silly pictures. Jim, who was upset at losing, believed him.

The night of a final both teams have a banquet and, of course, it has to go ahead win or lose. I'd had an invitation and had been told I could bring some friends so I turned up with two actors from *EastEnders*, Leslie Grantham ('Dirty Den') and Nejdep Salah (who played Ali the cafe owner). But when we got there the guy on the door let them in but said I couldn't go in.

'It's my invite,' I told him.

'Jim Gregory says you are not allowed in. Wait there.' A minute later this short, bald man who looked like Edward G. Robinson arrived at the door.

'Are you Eric Hall?' he asked. I told him that I was.

'Step outside. I'm going to have a fight with you, you lost me the Cup final with that players' pool. I know because so-and-so told me.'

'He's only a journalist, Jim, he doesn't know what happened.'

'Don't call me Jim, it's Mr Gregory to you.'

I thought he was just about to throw a punch when Jim Smith hauled him off. All the players who saw what was happening loved it, of course. 'Go on Jim, whack him!' they all shouted. Although I wasn't allowed in, I went for a drink in the bar and Leslie and Nejdep came out of the banquet to join me and so did most of the team.

Despite that bad start Jim Gregory and I later became friends when he moved to Portsmouth. Terry Venables was trying to take Darren Anderton from there to Spurs and I was involved in the negotiations because Paul Walsh, who was then at Tottenham, was part of the deal. Gregory kept telling Terry he didn't know what I was talking about. 'If he can't convince me he tries to confuse me,' he told him.

The next time the three of us were together I said to Gregory, 'Look Jim, it's simple. Spurs pay this, Darren gets that and Paul gets that. And boom, boom, boom, we've got a deal.' 'See what I mean,' said Gregory to Terry, 'he's doing it again. Just when I think I understand him he starts with this boom, boom, boom business. What the hell is that?'

I also organized the players' pool when Crystal Palace reached the FA Cup final in 1990 when they played Manchester United. I'm happy to say that in his autobiography Ian Wright, who then played for Palace, gave me some monster name checks saying that not only had he made money out of the pool but that thanks to Eric Hall he'd also had a lot of fun. Part of the pool was, as usual, the record. I wanted to have a new one written but the chairman insisted that they did the old Dave Clark Five hit 'Glad All Over' which had been adopted by the fans as the club song.

One of the plugs I'd organized was on the children's show *Blue Peter*. The team was supposed to turn up at the BBC studios in White City in a mini-bus I'd laid on. I'd left it to the three players who were on the pool committee, Ian Wright, Mark Bright and Gary O'Reilly, to make sure everyone was there. I was waiting at the studio when the coach arrived and the driver got off followed by Wright, Bright, O'Reilly and one other player who turned out to be Gareth Southgate plus a friend of Bright's who had come for the ride. 'Where are the others?' I asked Wrighty.

'Sorry Eric, they're not coming.'

'But bubbelah, there's supposed to be eleven in the team. I realize the producer is a bit camp and knows nothing about football but even he may work out that there are more than four players in a side.' In any case I'd done a deal with my Adidas mate Colin Wooldridge and we had to go ahead to get them a plug as part of the deal.

The interviewer was an old friend of mine, Peter Duncan, and he smelled a rat even if the producer didn't when Tony Hiller, who is over fifty, plus the coach driver, Mark Bright's friend, myself and the four players pretended to be the Crystal Palace team singing the song.

Somehow, with Peter Duncan's help I might add, we bluffed it out and, would you believe, I not only got one plug on that show, I got another one as a bonus the following week.

The programme *Points Of View*, then hosted by Peter Robinson, received a letter from a viewer saying that he'd seen the *Blue Peter* show in which the Crystal Palace team had appeared but instead of eleven players there were only eight and, of those, he only recognized four. Then they showed the clip of it again and gave us an extra plug.

Chapter Twenty-six

i had a very close call when I attempted to pull yet another stroke when I was doing the Wimbledon pool for their 1988 FA Cup Final against Liverpool. I had the idea of getting a picture of all the ladies involved with the players – it could be their wives, girlfriends, sisters or even mothers.

I called the sports editor of the *Today* newspaper and he thought it was a great idea for their features page. The women's editor loved it and I did a deal for a nice few quid for the picture which was to appear a couple of days before the final. All I had to do now was make sure the players delivered the goods – the ladies in their lives.

First of all I told the committee, which was Lawrie Sanchez, John Fashanu, Dennis Wise and John Scales, and they didn't have a problem. Then I told the rest of the team, 'I need a lady in your life, your wife, girlfriend, whatever, at the training ground on Sunday.' Then I heard a voice from the back say, 'There's no way that my lady is coming here.' It was big Eric Young, the central defender who I always thought was going to be a bit tricky. I loved him but, to be fair, he was sometimes a sausage short of a barbecue in my opinion. But I just hoped he'd relent.

When I arrived on the Sunday I was pleased to see at least six wives there, all in their best gear, plus a few girlfriends. The only player who hadn't sent anyone was Eric Young. I phoned him at home but he still refused to go along with us. So I thought 'Sod him' and I decided to put in a ringer. There was a lady who worked in the Wimbledon offices and I asked her to stand in as Eric's lady. The first thing that was wrong, I suppose, is that she was white and Eric's lady, like him, was coloured. The second thing was that the woman I chose was overweight. She was a lovely girl with a big personality but she was not very attractive, the sort of woman I associate with *Prisoner Cell Block H* if you get my meaning. But I didn't care, I was determined that *Today* would get it's money's worth.

So the picture appeared and everyone was happy, except Eric Young. I arrived at the training ground the day the picture was in the paper to be told by one of the players, 'Stay away from Eric Young if you want to live. He's fuming about that picture.' But I decided to brave it out and went to see the players after training. As I approached I heard a voice, that I have to say sounded very much like Terry Phelan's, shout out 'Here he comes Eric, take this and let him have it.' Suddenly I was confronted by the towering figure of Young waving a baseball bat and definitely intent on doing me some monster damage. I couldn't do it now but I swear I ran across that pitch so fast I think manager Bobby Gould considered putting me on the bench at Wembley.

The previous year I should have been involved with Tottenham in their players' pool for their FA Cup final against Coventry but I discovered that some people don't quite understand the meaning of the word democracy.

I had already been involved in an earlier Spurs pool and done well for them and with Steve Perryman, the captain, as one of my clients plus a few of the others in the team, I didn't anticipate any problem being appointed to represent them again. Steve told me that several

agents had put themselves forward but none of them were in my
league and he didn't expect any problems either. But when he rang
me after the meeting he sounded embarrassed. 'There's sort of good
news and bad news,' he said. 'You've got it but you haven't got it if
you know what I mean.'

I told him I didn't have a clue what he meant so he explained that
they'd had the first vote and I had won by fifteen votes to three.

'So what's the problem?' I asked.

'Well, the problem is that the three who voted against you, Glenn
Hoddle, Ray Clemence and Ossie Ardiles, wouldn't accept the deci-
sion and wanted another vote after lunch.'

It was clear that as senior players they would use the lunch hour
to try and influence some of the younger players to vote against me.

'So what happened?' I asked Steve later.

'The next vote you also won, this time by twelve votes to six.'

'So again, what's the problem?'

'They still wouldn't accept it and they reckon that if we have you
they will drop out and form their own pool,' said Steve.

In the end they didn't have a pool at all but they all did their own
thing individually – always a bad idea for the players who are not so
well known. I have to say it was another reason I had to dislike
Hoddle who I didn't like very much in the first place.

But if that was a low on the pool front a high which can never be
topped in my view came in 1986 when I brought off a unique double
by representing both teams in the final, and not just any old teams
but the Merseyside giants, Liverpool and Everton.

I had done the Everton pool in the previous two seasons when
they had met Watford and Manchester United at Wembley so when
they reached their third successive FA Cup final I figured they'd ask
me to join them again. I spoke to their captain Kevin Ratcliffe who
said they were having a meeting in the near future and he'd be in
touch. But as the weeks went by and nothing happened I began to

suspect that they'd gone to someone else. By now my second signing as a client, Paul Walsh, was an established player at Liverpool, so I asked him if they were interested in my services and he told me he'd have a talk with his captain, Alan Hansen. Two days later, Ratcliffe rang back and said, 'Sorry I've been so long but we've had loads of matches recently because of the fixtures pile-up and I couldn't get a meeting until yesterday. You are in again.'

I'd lost a lot of valuable time and got stuck in straight away, forgetting all about my call to Walshy. So when he rang back to say, 'Alan Hansen says he'd love you to do our pool,' I was a bit taken aback to say the least. I spluttered something about Everton asking me and Paul, rightly, did his nut. 'You'd better tell Alan that,' he said and the next thing I knew Hansen was on the line.

I tried to explain that it was my fault, not Paul's, and he was very nice about it but I was still amazed when Paul called again later that night and said, 'Ring Alan Hansen at home now.' I told Paul that everything was all right between Hansen and myself but all he said was 'Ring him now.' So I did and was amazed to hear what Hansen had to say.

'I've been having a chat with Kevin Ratcliffe and he says he doesn't mind if you do our pool as well as theirs. So how about it?' Despite the fact that I knew it was going to be the toughest task I'd ever taken on in football it was a challenge I couldn't turn my back on so I accepted.

Another remarkable twist was still to take place in this particular saga. Kenny Dalglish, Graeme Souness and a couple of the other senior Liverpool players suggested that the two teams share the same pool. It meant that all the money from the activities of the thirty or so players involved in the final went into one pot and that became a very big pot indeed. It also meant that the players just on the edge of the teams, those who were only substitutes, would be on a massive pay day by their standards.

I don't think anyone will ever again equal my 'double' of that year although I had another double later in the same summer when I handled the pool for both the England and Scotland World Cup teams. Needless to say, they didn't decide on a joint pool but it was still a great honour for me and I had a great time in Mexico shuttling between both squads of players.

Chapter Twenty-seven

i came into contact with Graeme Souness again a few years later when he became manager at Anfield after Kenny Dalglish quit the job. One of Souness's first priorities was to buy a central defender and the first player he wanted was one of my clients, John Scales at Wimbledon, but he was not for sale at the time. His second choice was also my man, Neil Ruddock who was then at Tottenham. Souness had already agreed terms with Spurs and Ruddock, his father-in-law Paul Bennett and myself were going to Liverpool to discuss wages, bonuses and all that stuff.

Souness invited us to hold the meeting at his own home and met us at Knutsford Service station to escort us to his magnificent home in Cheshire. Normally these deals are done at a hotel or restaurant or even at the club. Not only was this a very special setting but, I have to admit that when we walked into the dining room I was faced by one of the finest Jewish meals I'd ever seen.

I've been to Jewish weddings and barmitzvahs where they had less food. I hadn't realized that Graeme's lovely lady was Jewish and when she knew that I was visiting she decided to make me feel welcome, or perhaps Graeme decided that the way to a Jewish

141

agent's heart is through his stomach. There was pickled herring, shmaltz herring, gefiltafish, both boiled and fried, which you seldom see together, salmon, salt beef, chopped liver and a monster array of genuine Jewish food that makes the mouth water even as I write about it.

As far as I was concerned Graeme could have had anything he wanted but I still had to do the best possible deal for my client which turned out to be very difficult in the circumstances, not because of Liverpool but because of the problems caused by Tottenham.

Liverpool chairman David Moores and that lovely secretary Peter Robinson joined us for the meal and after several hours of negotiation the deal was done – or so we thought. The next morning – we'd stayed the night after such a long, hard day of negotiating and eating – a fax arrived at Anfield from Tottenham saying that they would not release Ruddock unless he agreed to waive his right to a loyalty payment that was owed to him.

There was only one answer to that as far as I was concerned and it consisted of two words: the first started with 'f' and the second was 'off'. Their response to that came from Ossie Ardiles, who was now their manager. He said that he was not happy with the deal and if Ruddock refused to sign the waiver he would increase the transfer fee by a couple of hundred grand.

Now that was outrageous. Once a figure has been agreed between clubs there is no way that either of them can go back on it after the player has agreed terms and Liverpool were rightly angry with Tottenham. Souness was particularly upset because he was desperate to get Neil. I was told by another member of the Liverpool staff that he actually offered to pay the extra money out of his own pocket and then recoup the money when Ruddock was sold at a later date.

The situation still hadn't been resolved by the evening so Neil stayed on, hoping to sign the following day, and Paul Bennett and myself returned to London. We were in one of those big Range Rovertype vehicles where you can stretch out and I woke up at about 1 am still monster unhappy about the way Tottenham were behaving.

I decided to ring Ardiles at home. When he picked up the phone it was obvious he was in bed.

'Who's that?' he shouted.

'Is that you Ossie?'

'Yes. Who is this ringing so late?'

'It's Eric Hall.'

'Why are you ringing so very, very late?' 'Never mind that, what the f***'s going on with the Ruddock transfer?'

'Don't you use language like that to me. You are very, very bad person. I am only doing what Mr Sugar tells me to do.'

That was Tottenham chairman Alan Sugar and Ardiles was sounding like one of those men in the Nuremberg trials – 'I vas only obeying orders'. He slammed the phone down on me so I waited a few minutes and then phoned him again.

'Hello, who's that?'

'It's Eric Hall.'

'I told you already it's very, very late. You very, very bad man doing this to me and my family.'

'I'm not the bad man. You are, you schmuck. You phone Liverpool in the morning and let the deal go through or I'll make your life hell.'

'Don't you threaten me you very, very bad man.'

I swear I rang him five more times in the next fifteen minutes and every time he answered before slamming the phone down. So the next time I rang and he answered I said, 'Listen I've got a suggestion to make.'

'No, no you very, very bad man. I won't talk about Ruddock no more.'

But before he could slam the phone down again I said, 'Do yourself a favour, Ossie.'

'What's that?'

'This time take the phone off the hook.'

The deal did eventually go through but Paul and I still have a chuckle about that night. I thought about it again when I met an Argentinian waiter at Terry Venables' club Scribes. He had been working as a temp but one day was given a full-time job. So I said to him, 'That's good news for you, Carlos.'

'Yes, I'm very, very happy, Mr Hall, to be working at this wonderful club with all these very, very wonderful people.'

'By the way, where did you work before?' 'I work at Blates.'

'Blates? Never heard of it.'

'Oh yes, Mr Hall, very, very famous hotel Blates.'

'Sorry Carlos, it's a new one on me.'

'You know the actress Anouska Hempel is there.'

'Oh! You mean Blakes Hotel.'

'That's right Blates Hotel, very, very good. Lots of famous people. Last week there was very big birthday party for John Hollins.'

'Really. I'm surprised Terry Venables wasn't there. He and John Hollins go back a long way.'

'Yes, very nice person John Hollins. Everyone was there you know. Mr Frank Sinatra, Roger Moore, all the stars at this party.'

'Are you sure? I know John Hollins is a lovely person but I can't see Frank Sinatra flying in for his party.'

'Yes, Frank Sinatra was there. I see him. Also Prince Charles and Princess Diana.'

I turned to Tel and said, 'Have you heard this? John Hollins who you used to play with had a party at Blakes and Sinatra and Charles and Di and everyone in the world is there except you.'

'There's no way,' said Venables. 'Are you making this up, Carlos?'

'No, I swear. From the very, very famous television programme, *Dynasty*.'

And Terry, his wife Toots and myself all said together, 'Ah! Not John Hollins but Joan Collins.'

Talking about Scribes reminds me of the Christmas lunch Tel, then manager of Tottenham (everyone seems to be Tottenham manager at some time or other) gave for the players on the one day when they were allowed to let their hair down before the busy playing programme over the Christmas period.

I used to run the karaoke at the club and Terry asked me to organize one for the lads. When I arrived I noticed that Paul Gascoigne, the Geordie star of the team and already a recognized hell raiser, was missing. I asked Terry where he was and he explained that he was doing a commercial and would arrive later. By the time Gazza arrived all the other players were well on their way to being merry – with the boss's approval on this special occasion.

So he decided to catch up in a hurry. He went to the bar and started ordering drink after drink. He was knocking them back so fast that the barman Nick couldn't keep up with him. Pretty soon not only had he caught up with the rest of the players but he'd rapidly overtaken them, to the extent that he was well plastered. So Nick, a lovely barman who has been there, seen it and done it in all the top hotels and clubs in London's West End, decided it was time to call a halt. He called Terry over and said, 'I'm sorry, Mr Venables, but I think Mr Gascoigne might just have had a little too much to drink.' Terry took one look at Gazza and agreed. 'Don't serve him any more and if he argues tell him to see me,' he said.

Within minutes Gazza was back at the bar demanding another drink. 'I'm sorry sir, I can't serve you with any more drink.'

'What do you mean? Just one more.'

'No sir, I have had instructions from Mr Venables, no more. If you want to complain you must see him.'

'I'll tell you what,' said Gazza. 'If you don't give me another drink I'll make sure you never work in Newcastle.'

To which Nick replied, 'I think I can live with that, sir.'

Here's another quick story about my karaoke experiences at

Scribes. Someone brought East End gangster 'Mad' Frankie Fraser to the club one night. I spotted him and, being incapable of thinking before talking, said, 'Come on, Frankie, sing us a song.'

'No. I don't know any songs,' he replied.

'Of course you do. There's "If I Had A Hammer" and that great Elton John number "Don't Go Breaking My Legs". Try one of those.'

Frankie Fraser laughed it off but Terry Venables didn't. If Frankie's presence didn't please him too much, me taking the mickey was even worse.

Chapter Twenty-eight

I'm glad to say that despite the cut-throat nature of the football business with transfers and negotiating contracts, I've made more friends than enemies since I became an agent. And I've had far more laughs than heartaches thanks to those friends whether they were managers, players or chairmen.

I can't mention them all but there are some memories that are outstanding. One of the managers concerned was David Webb, formerly a great player and always a monster funny man. I received a call one day from a German television company who wanted to do a programme about a day in the life of Eric Hall. They said that what they really wanted to do was come with me to a football match. This was on a Friday afternoon and they wanted to do it the following day.

I said to them, 'Are you mad? You can't just ring up Chelsea, Arsenal or whatever and tell them to make room for a German TV crew at twenty-four hours' notice.' Then I thought of my mate David Webb who was then manager of Brentford, a lovely club where I had two players, Martin Grainger and Nicky Forster, and where the arrival of a TV crew wouldn't cause a panic. But if you put David Webb and myself together anything can happen and usually does.

And it did this time. The Germans filmed me watching the game and although as usual I didn't have a clue what was happening, I did notice that my boy Forster scored a hat-trick so it was a good story for them. Unfortunately for me I had been vigorously trying to sell both Forster and Grainger for weeks with stories in the press saying such-and-such a club were in for this one and so-and-so was in for that one. The supporters were aware of what I was up to but I didn't realize how unhappy they were about it until the TV crew suggested that they took some shots of me in the executive members' club where some of the wealthier supporters go after the match. I boldly marched into the club only to find a dartboard in the bar with my picture in the middle and some large, angry men throwing darts at it. They couldn't believe it when they saw me in person and I had to beat a hasty retreat and run as fast as I had when Eric Young was chasing me.

There was worse to come when they decided to interview David Webb. All afternoon I'd been giving him that old line about 'not mentioning the war' because it was a German TV station. But I didn't really think he'd drop me in it. I should have remembered his warped sense of humour. They asked him what he thought about me and he told them the usual stuff: 'He drives me potty but I wish I had had him as my agent when I was a player', etc. I stood there looking pleased with myself. Then they asked him to talk about the players he'd known during his career at Chelsea and QPR. He mentioned guys like Rodney Marsh, Terry Venables, Peter Osgood and Alan Hudson and then he said with a straight face, 'But my favourite player of all was Bomber Harris.' The interview was abruptly halted and the producer gave me a strange look and asked if this was a joke. While Webby walked away killing himself with laughter I was left trying to explain that Bomber is the nickname for everyone named Harris in England and the player he was talking about was that great defender Ron Harris of Chelsea. But I don't think he believed me and

I couldn't blame him because Ron Harris's nickname was actually 'Chopper' and everyone, especially David, knew that.

Another great character and friend who I have had so much fun dealing with is Harry Redknapp, a former West Ham player who took over as manager when Billy Bonds left. Last season I was re-negotiating John Moncur's contract at Upton Park. Harry and myself met in chief executive Peter Storey's office, which overlooks a council estate. It's a typical East London estate with TV aerials and satellite dishes on every roof, washing hanging from the balconies and rubbish all over the place. Harry told me about the day he had sat in the same office negotiating a deal with the Romanian international Florin Raducioiu who was with his agent and an interpreter. The money side of the deal had been agreed when the agent asked about accommodation for his player. Harry told them through the interpreter that, while he was looking for a house, they could put him up in one of the apartments they owned. The interpreter told the player this and he looked happy enough. Then he asked where the flats were and Harry, unable to resist temptation, pointed to the dingy block he could see out of the window. 'It's them,' he said. The interpreter told the Romanian what he had said and Harry was about to explain that it was just a little joke when the interpreter told him:

'Florin says that is very good because he won't need a car, he can walk to work.' Harry told me, and he swears it's true, that Raducioiu was actually disappointed when he was taken to the real apartments which were very posh places in Chigwell.

I also have a monster soft spot for David Pleat who has been manager at Luton, Tottenham and Sheffield Wednesday. We had a very stormy start to our relationship which began when I became Paul Walsh's agent. When Walsh and his father informed David Pleat, who was his manager at Luton, that I would be handling all the negotiations for Paul's transfer to Liverpool he went crazy. He phoned me and began shouting and screaming, 'I'm David Pleat, the manager of

Luton, who the bloody hell do you think you are? I've never heard of you before, what other clients have you got? I want to see you, get here right away.'

Perhaps because I was new to the game I agreed to meet him, whereas today I'd have told him, 'You want to see me, you come here.' So I went to Luton the following day and met David and a man called Doc Berry, who was the club's physio and also happened to be the father of Paul Walsh's girlfriend of the time.

David Pleat was still very aggressive and asked, 'What can you do for Paul that I can't do.'

'Well, I can be his agent for a start which you can't because you're the manager,' I told him.

He then said, 'I've already got him the best possible deal with Liverpool so why does he need you?' That's when it was my turn to snap. 'You've done a deal! How dare you interfere? And how dare Liverpool tell you what they'll pay Paul without even discussing it with him?' I think he realized then that he was on dodgy ground and he calmed down a bit.

But it wasn't the end of our feud because soon after Luton reached the semi-final of the 1989 League Cup where they would play West Ham and not only was I doing the players' pool but I was invited by the chairman David Kohler, who I had got on very well with, to be his personal guest in the directors' box. I went with a good friend of mine, Ted Buxton, and we were sitting in the restaurant an hour before the match when in walked David, wearing his tracksuit. The rest of the people in the restaurant couldn't believe it – apparently they'd never seen him in there prior to a match. He walked straight over to me and Ted and yelled, 'What are you doing here. How did you get a ticket?' I told him the chairman had invited us. 'That's it, I'm resigning,' he said. 'I wanted a ticket for my son but I couldn't even buy one and you are getting in for nothing. I'm going to see the chairman, I'm not standing for it.' Off he went, still shouting and hollering, and Ted and I took our seat in the stand.

Suddenly David appeared on the touchline, looked up and saw us in the directors' box. He jumped over the wall and ran up the terracing. 'Ted, come here I want to talk to you in private,' he said. He and Ted then walked around the pitch and I could see that David was very animated. Remember, this is about five minutes before the kick-off of a Cup semi-final. When Ted returned I asked him what it was all about. 'He's still threatening to resign. He says he hates the chairman and the club and he hates you even more.'

Luton won the match and so would play the final against Arsenal at Wembley. As I was doing the pool for them I wanted to congratulate the players. Ted and I had a pass for the players' bar so down we went. One of David Pleat's assistants was on the door. 'Hello Ted, nice to see you,' he said, ushering him in. Then he looked at me and said, 'You can't come in here.'

'What do you mean? I've got a pass.'

'It's invalid for this match.'

'Well, Ted's got the same pass.'

'That's different, I know who he is I don't know who you are.'

'But I have to see the players.'

'I don't care. I've had strict instructions from Mr Pleat that you are not allowed to go anywhere near the players.'

'You just said you didn't know who I was.'

'Well, I do know who you are, you're a troublemaker and you can't come in.'

And so it went on until one of the players, Ceri Hughes, came out and saw me. 'Hello Monster, great isn't it? You coming in?'

I told him that the jobsworth on the door wouldn't let me in. 'Right, wait there,' he said. He went back into the bar and came out with about seven other players. 'If you can't come in we're not staying either,' he said. 'Let's go to the pub over the road and talk business.' And off we went, leaving the bloke on the door speechless at last.

Eventually David and I made it up and became good friends but I have to say he is the only manager I've ever dealt with who actually talked in pence. It was when I was working out the deal for Phil Gray's move from Tottenham to Luton. There are many parts to a transfer – wages, win bonuses, the bonus for winning championships and Cups, the loyalty payments and boom, boom, boom, but they all have one thing in common, or they do with most people. They are all settled in pounds sterling. It's £100 for that, £200 for this and maybe £70 for whatever. Not with David it wasn't. 'We'll pay £22.63 for every point we get while he's in the team,' and £61.47 for this and £94.55 for that. He has since told me that he was only joking and he's such a lovely man I'm not going to call him a liar, ish.

One manager who is not a fan of mine, as I discovered a few years ago, is Manchester United's Alex Ferguson. I had made a video called *Eric Hall's Monster Hits* in which I set up people in football in a sort of *You've Been Framed*-type situation and the producer decided to do a Vox Pops – interviewing people to get their opinions about me.

It so happened that a week or so after he mentioned it the Football Writers annual dinner was being held at the Royal Lancaster and as I had been invited to attend we decided it was an ideal opportunity to interview all the managers and players who were present. The producer got permission to send a camera crew and an interviewer and they went around asking people what they thought about Eric Hall. Most of them said nice things about me until they got to Alex Ferguson. He was at the dinner because Eric Cantona, one of his players at Old Trafford, had been voted Footballer of the Year. So when the interviewer went to him and asked, 'Can we have a chat about Eric,' he thought they meant Cantona not Hall. He was charming and tidied himself up before standing in front of the camera and putting on his best smile.

CHAPTER TWENTY-EIGHT

'Well, Alex, tell us what you think about Eric Hall?'

'Eric Hall? F*** off,' he said, and stormed out. Obviously he's one guy I haven't actually won over yet.

Chapter Twenty-nine

I 've mentioned some of the chairmen with whom I've got on well and there are a few that I haven't but there are those of whom I have very special memories. Among those is Chelsea's Ken Bates, not everyone's favourite man I know, but we have always spoken the same language and I am full of praise for the way he operates and for what he has done for the club. The ground is now ultra-modern with a luxury hotel and fine stands but when I first dealt with Ken it was in a hut in the car park. The second time I re-negotiated Dennis Wise's contract it was in an office but it was still a bit run down.

I was my usual aggressive self, giving it the full works. 'I want this and that and the other,' and Ken was equally tough. 'No way can you have that, otherwise every player will want it,' and so on and so forth. Normally we found a compromise but when we got to one particular point we couldn't agree on I said to Dennis, 'That's it we are going home. I'm sorry Ken, I love you but I can't do this deal. No way.' I then made a dramatic exit, slamming the door behind me, only to discover I'd walked into a broom cupboard and was surrounded by dusters and tins of polish. It was about three feet wide and five feet deep and there was no way for me to go except back the way I came. So I turned around and opened the door and there was Ken Bates, Colin Hutchinson his managing director and Dennis all falling about laughing.

I said something stupid to try and cover my embarrassment and it broke the ice. Ken said, 'Now come on Eric sit down and let's look at this problem. I'll tell you what I can do. I can pay what you want but not in the way you've asked for, I'll do it in another way but it works out the same.' I went off the handle again. 'I told you Ken I can't accept that. You're not listening.' 'I'm telling you I agree to it,' he said when I finally finished. 'I agreed to it twenty minutes ago but you are the only agent I know who can't take "yes" for an answer.'

On another occasion Ken phoned me to ask, 'Are you Dennis Bergkamp's agent?' I told him I wasn't.

'I didn't think so but I've just had someone on who sounded like you and said he was you. He also said he represented Bergkamp and asked if I wanted to buy him.'

'What did you tell him?' I asked.

'I told him to eff off because I knew he wasn't Eric Hall.'

'What made you so sure it wasn't me?'

'Because I understood every word he said.' Nice one Ken.

Another top man in football is Wimbledon's Sam Hammam. Dealing with Sam is an amazing experience because he is such an emotional man. I usually go to his beautiful house in the St John's Wood area of London to discuss our business and his lovely wife brings out fruit and sandwiches and makes a fuss of me and he gives me a hug. Then we start talking about a deal and I'll say something like, 'Now come on Sam, you know this player is worth more than that.'

And he'll go crazy. He says, 'How dare you say that to me, you little b*****d,' and then he starts punching me and shouting over and over, 'You b*****d, you b*****d. I am your uncle, your brother, your father but you insult me.'

'No Sam, I'm not your nephew, your brother or your son. I'm an agent and I'm here to talk about money for my player.'

'No Eric, you are family and I love you. We must not argue about money.'

Sam is just trying to talk me out of what I'm there to do but he's a wonderful man who gave me one of my proudest moments in football after Wimbledon played Liverpool in that 1988 FA Cup final. Bobby Gould and his team of so-called no-hopers won that match and there was a monster victory celebration at a Wimbledon hotel.

The BBC did their *Match Of The Day* programme live from the hotel during which Sam made a very rare mistake. He went on air live and said, 'This victory changes nothing. We are still a family as far as I'm concerned and if any of my players are unhappy they can knock on my door tomorrow and I will let them go.'

Whoops! That's all I wanted to hear because I had Dennis Wise, then with the Dons, John Fashanu, Andy Thorne and goalkeeper Dave Beasant all being chased by top teams with a fortune waiting for them. So a couple of days later, at my instigation, all four of them went in to see Bobby Gould to ask for a move.

'What are you talking about? We've just won the Cup, we're all together. You can't leave,' said Bobby.

They replied, 'But Sam said if we were not happy he'd let us go,' and Bobby had no answer. Eventually they all moved on but Sam made monster sure he got a fortune for all of them.

Anyway, I was shattered by the time of the party because it had been a hectic five weeks organizing the players' pool. (Sam hadn't always been happy with what I was doing so I had received a lot of punches during that spell.) I was just about to leave the party when Sam said, 'Where are you staying tonight?'

'I'm going home,' I told him.

'No, you must not go home. You can't drive because you've been drinking and anyway you have to be back here at seven o'clock in the morning.'

'Are you mad? All I want to do tomorrow morning is sleep.'

'No you must come and sit next to me on the bus.'

'Bus, what bus?'

'The bus that will carry all the players and staff through Wimbledon with the Cup to the Town Hall,' said Sam.

I was speechless as I realized that I really was family and that Sam did genuinely feel about me the way he said. It was a fantastic feeling as I sat next to him on that bus with the thousands of fans lining the street. I even finished up lifting the trophy above my head like one of the players as we stood on the Town Hall balcony. I'd been with Terry Venables and Tottenham when they had lost in the final against Coventry the previous year but being with the winners and in such a privileged position was incredible.

Some years later the lovely actress June Whitfield, who is a monster huge Wimbledon supporter, met me at a showbiz function and asked, 'I've seen you at Wimbledon. You lifted the Cup that year in the Town Hall. What is your job there?' When I told her I was just an agent she was gobsmacked. 'I've been a fan for years but they wouldn't have let me on the bus,' she said.

Another of my favourite football personalities is that very special lady Karren Brady, the chief executive of Birmingham City. She is married to one of City's former players, Paul Peschisolido, and I was delighted to be invited to the wedding. I had first met Paul when he was a player for Canadian club Toronto Blizzard and I was the one who called to tell him that Karren Brady wanted him to give her a ring because she fancied him. I meant that she fancied him as a player and the ring was a telephone call but as it turned out she later fancied him as a husband and the ring was that band of gold.

Like a schmuck I forgot to turn off my mobile phone during the wedding ceremony and right in the middle of it all I got a call.

'Hang on Paul,' I shouted, 'don't say yes yet, it might be Liverpool on for you.'

Since they were married Paul has had transfers to Stoke and Fulham and it seems that wherever he has gone Karren has found a house she likes in the area before agreeing to the transfer. It's as Paul said to me: 'Monster, maybe you should have been my estate agent, I think you'd have made more money.'

Chapter Thirty

i 've had lots of laughs as an agent but I think one of the funniest incidents concerned Francis Lee. He had the misfortune to have me on the other side of the negotiating table when he signed his first player after taking over as chairman at Manchester City. The player was Paul Walsh, who keeps cropping up in this book mainly because he had more moves than Pickfords. This time he was moving to City from Portsmouth and was joining them on the recommendation of City's manager Brian Horton, who had played with Paul at Luton. I bet Francis had wished he'd looked elsewhere after I'd had him on the rack for over eight hours.

We met in the Mottram Hall Hotel near Manchester and Francis turned up looking immaculate. By the time we'd finished doing the deal he looked like the Herbert Lom character in the Pink Panther films, the one Clouseau drives totally mad. His tie was all twisted, his shirt was soaking wet, he had a twitch, he was talking to himself and he looked a nervous wreck. I had argued about everything and pushed the wages higher by the hour. But finally we got there.

Paul was staying overnight for a medical and I was being driven back to London but before we went we had a final bottle of champagne to celebrate the deal. Francis said, 'I'm desperate for a smoke after all that, can I have one of your small cigars?'

'No, have one of my monster Churchill-size Romeo Y Julieta cigars,' I said.

'All right, I'll have a small one now and a big one for later,' he replied and for the first time during the day he started laughing.

'I've finally done you,' he chortled, 'I've got two cigars out of you for nothing.'

He was definitely in a bad way but we parted as friends and I settled down for a sleep on the journey home. It must have been about 2 am when my mobile phone rang.

It was Francis Lee. 'Hello again, bubbelah, what's the problem?' I asked, thinking he was about to pull out of the deal.

'Eric, as you know I've been a player, I've been a successful businessman and a racehorse trainer but this is my first transfer deal as a chairman and my first experience of football agents. I have to know something, are they all like you?' 'I hope not,' I told him. 'I'd like to think I was unique.'

'Thank heavens for that, I don't think I could handle any more days like today.'

'Is that all you called for?'

'No, I called to let you know that the trick worked.'

'What trick?'

'Well, I got home and my wife had left me some lovely smoked salmon sandwiches. So I ate those then I settled down to relax with a little drink and I remembered that big cigar you gave me.'

'I thought, I know I've paid far too much money for your player but, what the hell, life's too short to worry about it, so enjoy yourself Francis.'

'I lit the cigar, blew out a big puff of smoke and then bang! The bloody thing exploded. It was so loud the kids woke up, the dog started barking, the cat jumped out of the window, the wife came rushing downstairs. All hell was let loose so I thought I'd ring you to let you know that you'd won again.'

I honestly didn't know what he was talking about but I discovered the next day what had happened when I went to Scribes to see Terry Venables who asked, 'Enjoyed your cigars this week?' He explained that his wife Toots, who is a great practical joker, had taken one of my cigars out of my jacket pocket while I was doing the karaoke and put one of those exploding pellets into the end of the cigar. She'd been waiting all night for me to light it, it was like playing Russian roulette, but I'd managed to avoid that particular cigar which turned out to be the one I gave Francis Lee.

After that experience I'm surprised he lasted as long as he did before getting out. Brian Horton left Manchester City before him, of course, and was replaced by the lovely Alan Ball. I called him during his first week and asked him if he wanted to sell Paul Walsh – he was due another move by then I reckoned.

'I'll sell anyone,' said Alan.

'Why is that?'

'I arrived at the training ground this morning just as the players were coming back from a cross-country run. And as I stood watching them come over the hill I knew how General Custer must have felt at the Little Big Horn.'

'What do you mean?'

'Like the Red Indians, they just kept coming and coming. There's hundreds of them, Monster, so yes, I'll sell Paul Walsh and about thirty others.'

Another chairman I had a funny experience with was Bill Fox who was at Blackburn before Jack Walker took over. Only this was funny peculiar not funny ha, ha. It was 1990 and I was acting for Tottenham goalkeeper Bobby Mimms. For three weeks I'd been talking to the Blackburn manager Don Mackay in order to put the transfer together. Finally the clubs agreed a price and I went with

Bobby to Ewood Park to sort out his contract.

When we arrived the receptionist told Bobby that he was expected, then she looked at me and said, 'And who is this gentleman?'

'It's my agent, Eric Hall,' he told her.

She phoned Don Mackay and said, 'It's Bobby Mimms and Eric Hall to see you.' Although I didn't witness this, I was told later by his assistant that Mackay went white with fright when he heard I was about. He came out and asked me what I was doing there.

'I can't talk to you, it's against the rules to talk to agents.'

'Let's go then, Bobby,' I said.

'No, be reasonable,' said Don. 'You can wait outside and if Bobby needs to discuss anything with you he can go out and see you.'

And he was serious. Bobby then stepped in and said, 'How did you find out that I was available in the first place, wasn't it because Eric told you?'

'Well, yes we did chat and he did mention your name,' said Mackay.

'But now you won't talk to him to discuss my terms. I'm sorry, if he's not allowed in the meeting then I don't sign.'

By now Mackay was panicking so he decided to ring Bill Fox, who apart from being the Blackburn chairman was also president of the Football League. I could hear him saying that I was with Bobby Mimms and that it was against the rules and boom, boom, boom. Then he said to me, 'Mr Fox wants to talk to you.'

Now older readers will know what I mean when I say that Bill Fox was like Snudge in the TV programme, *Bootsy And Snudge*. He looked just like the actor Bill Fraser – same little moustache and talked exactly like him. He also told me they were not expecting me.

'But you arranged the flight for us and the tickets were booked in the names of Mimms and Hall so you knew I was coming,' I told him.

'Yes, but we didn't expect you to attend the meeting.'

'What did you think I was going to do, carry his bags?'

Eventually he suggested a compromise. 'It says in the rules that we must not meet with an agent, so if we do the deal over the phone I can honestly say we've never met.'

And that's what we did, but if you think that was crazy there was an even dafter end to the saga. Without any prompting from me, Mr Fox paid me £17,500 for being so helpful in the transfer dealings. I suppose some people would say that was a 'bung' – the word used to describe illegal payments in the football business – and as it came from the League president it would have caused a storm had it been made public at the time.

But I didn't regard it as a 'bung'. He was happy with the deal and he wanted to show his appreciation. It was a gift as far as I was concerned, not an incentive.

I once bought Terry Venables a satellite TV system as a Christmas gift. It wasn't a payment or an incentive to get more business, but a gift to a good friend.

Chapter Thirty-one

One of my favourite characters in football was Stan Flashman, who bought the Barnet club. He was a lovely man who was always straight with me. Unfortunately he got into financial bother and all the Barnet players became free agents, which did me no harm at all.

I had their top striker Gary Bull – the cousin of the Wolves player Steve Bull – as a client and he was a hot property at the time with lots of speculation in the press about Arsenal, Spurs and many other top clubs wanting him. But the club that had moved in with a bid the previous season was Nottingham Forest, managed by Brian Clough. By the time Gary had become a free agent Cloughie had left and Frank Clark, another good friend of mine, had taken over. Frank contacted me as soon as he heard about the situation at Barnet. He also spoke to Gary and gave him some idea of what he would get if he joined Forest. We arranged to go and meet Frank and the club chairman Fred Reacher the following day. Again my old friend Ted Buxton travelled with us and when we stopped at one of the M1 service stations my mobile phone rang.

It was Graeme Souness, the Liverpool manager. 'Eric, is it true that Gary Bull is having talks with Forest today?'

I told him we were on our way. 'I want him,' said Graeme. 'We can do a deal here and now.' I put all the obstacles up I could think of to slow things down – not because I didn't want Gary to join Liverpool but because we'd promised Frank Clark that we'd talk to him first.

'He'll want such-and-such money at least,' I said.

'He's got it,' said Graeme.

'Forest have agreed to let him have a house rent free for eighteen months,' I added.

'We'll give it to him for two years,' replied Graeme.

I was very tempted and Gary, sitting in the back, could hear what I was saying. He told me that he had always been a Liverpool fan and would love to join them. But, to his eternal credit, he added, 'I have given my word that I will talk to Mr Clark and even though I will probably live to regret it, I am not going to break that promise.'

My mind was still working out how much more a move to Liverpool would be worth. I didn't exactly try and talk Gary out of joining Forest but when we arrived there was a coloured lad painting the gates. A week before Forest had signed Stan Collymore for a lot of money and this lad was the spitting image of him so I said to Gary, 'See what sort of club they are. It may be the summer but they still make their star players earn their money.' But he wouldn't budge and after talking to Frank he joined them.

I used the fact that Souness had phoned us to frighten Forest into giving Gary a monster deal, which was only fair because a year earlier they'd offered Barnet £1 million for him and now they were getting him for nothing.

After we'd done the deal Frank's assistant Alan Hill called me over and said, 'The chairman Fred Reacher is so happy that we've done the deal and that you've been so honest with us he wants to give you a plate.'

'Are you sure! Don't you think he could buy me a bunch of flowers or maybe take me for a meal first.'

'No, a commemorative plate, you schmuck.'

The chairman told me as we left that he'd never dealt with an agent before. 'Brian Clough always insisted that he handled all the transfer deals personally,' he said.

Yes, and I think we all now know why Cloughie was so insistent.

Gary Bull's honest approach is the norm with most of the footballers I've dealt with but there have been some who surprised me and some who have let me down. I won't go too deeply into some of the stories for legal reasons but I have to say that I was really disappointed by one of my clients, Gary Blissett. I had loaned Gary a large sum of money – well, it was large for an East End Jewish boy at £25,000-ish. He already owed me payment from a transfer deal I had arranged when he had appealed to me saying that his mother had died and that he had no money to cover the funeral expenses. I gave him a large sum but discovered later that it was about the third time she had died and others had paid for her funeral before and after me.

On another occasion he turned up on Christmas Eve saying he'd been let down by someone who owed him money and he had no cash to buy food or presents for his wife and kids. Again I finished up in tears after listening to his sob story and handed over a large wad.

Before I realized that I'd been conned Gary was granted a free transfer by Wimbledon and, as his agent, I started looking for clubs for him. I figured that if I could get him a good deal I'd get my cash back. I spoke to clubs like Watford, Luton, Crystal Palace and Wycombe Wanderers who all showed interest.

Then Gary called me to say that another agent was offering to organize a transfer to a club in China. Thinking that if he got the deal I would at least get my money back, I told Gary that I was happy to let him deal with another party, as long as he kept me informed.

A week or so went by and I hadn't heard anything so I rang Gary. His wife Debbie answered.

CHAPTER THIRTY-ONE

'He's not here,' she said. 'He's gone to China.'

'What? Do you mean he's gone to a Chinese for a take away?'

'No, he flew to China yesterday to sign for a team.'

I couldn't believe my ears. They'd done the deal and no-one had told me. Gary had disappeared without paying me back the money he owed me. Eventually I had to take Gary to court to get back the money I was owed.

I have also been amazed to discover that when it comes to cash there is very little loyalty between members of the same family, even twin brothers. I once did a picture deal with a newspaper involving the twins Dean and David Holdsworth. Dean was the bigger star – playing for Wimbledon at the time – and David was a lesser light at Watford. The deal was only for £2,000 but when I mentioned it to Dean he said, 'Send me all the money and I'll pay David. And if he asks tell him we only got £1,000.' He wasn't my client for much longer after that.

I was also staggered by an incident involving the Fashanu brothers, John and Justin. I'd been John's agent for many years but had never acted for Justin so I was surprised to get a call from him one day when he was living in Canada.

'I've got a problem, and I want you to help me,' he said.

He told me that a Sunday tabloid had obtained compromising pictures of him in a gay bar and they were going to expose him as a homosexual the following week. I asked him to level with me. 'I don't care if you are gay or not. I've even had a pop star write a love song for me so I'm not shocked. But I need to know the truth in order to help you.'

He then admitted that he was gay and had been actively so for many years, even when he was playing at the top level for Norwich and Nottingham Forest. I had an idea forming in my mind but I told him I'd call him back. I then called Kelvin Mackenzie, who was then the editor of the *Sun* newspaper and told him what Justin had told me. I suggested that his paper should carry an exclusive interview with Justin in which he would confess that he was homosexual. That way the gay bar pictures wouldn't matter any more. I also had a feeling, although he didn't tell me this, that Justin was being black-mailed so a confession would get rid of that problem as well.

Kelvin liked the idea. We waited until that Sunday to make sure the other newspaper hadn't run the story and were waiting for the following week as Justin had said, then the *Sun* sent one of their reporters to Canada to meet Justin and bring him back to London where they put him up in the Waldorf Hotel.

I had done a deal that was bringing Justin £100,000, less my commission of course, and I thought I'd done the kid a favour. Nothing had changed, he would be publicly revealed as being gay whichever story ran, and it was better coming from his own mouth. But his brother John didn't think so because the following day he called me to say, 'Pull the story, it musn't go in.'

I asked why not and he told me, 'Can you imagine what it will be like for me when the fans read that my brother is gay. They'll give me hell.'

I told him that I thought that was a very selfish attitude. 'How much is he getting?' he asked.

'You ask him, I'm not telling you.'

He called back to say, 'I know it's £100,000 but if you pull the story I'll pay Justin and you out of my own pocket.'

I explained that the money was not important, it was the only way to solve Justin's problem and anyhow the *Sun* had spent too much time and effort on it now and they wouldn't pull out even if I asked them to. I'd also signed a contract and anyhow, suppose they did pull it. The Sunday tabloid story would put Justin in an even worse light. John refused to listen and just kept on telling me what it would do to him. He said that if the story did appear he would never work with me again. So much for brotherly love.

The *Sun* did carry the story and as he threatened John and I never worked together again. I didn't even hear from John again but I did get another call from Justin some years later. I had been in hospital and my assistant Tony Maskell was listing all the phone messages that had piled up during my absence.

'There was so-and-so and this one, that one and there was also a call from Justin Fashanu. He asked you to phone him urgently.'

I didn't know exactly when Justin had called but I had the number, and I recognised the Canadian code. I decided not to call then because of the time difference. It would have been in the middle of the night in Canada so I put it off until the next day. But there was no next day for Justin because I had a call from someone at Radio Five the following morning saying that Justin had been found dead in a garage in East London. I was stunned because I couldn't help thinking that if I had been in the office when he rang I might have been able to do or say something that would have meant he would still be alive today.

I don't suppose I'll ever find the answer to that question and neither will I ever figure out how football families seem so distant to each other. The famous Allen clan, consisting of Clive, Paul, Martin and Bradley – all top players during the last fifteen years – and before them Les, the father of Clive and Bradley, and Dennis, was not a close family. I think they hardly ever talked to each other. I was once offered £10,000 by a football magazine who wanted a picture of them all together but Clive refused to even consider it.

I was the agent for Clive, Paul and Martin at various times and Clive was another of my players who upset me with his attitude. He had a fantastic season when he was with me as he scored over fifty goals for Tottenham but he had a great year off the field as well with the commercial work I got him. Then one day I had a call out of the blue from Clive asking me to meet him at the Royal Lancaster hotel that afternoon. When I turned up he told me, 'I've been to see my accountant and do you realize that in the past year you earned me £250,000.'

I told him I did know that because I'd worked my cobblers off getting him that much.

'Yes, but my accountant also told me that your 20 per cent earned you £50,000.'

I told him to congratulate his accountant on being able to work that out so quickly, but I knew what the bottom line was going to be.

'Well I've been thinking that as of next season I'll give you only 15 per cent.'

I told him, 'Funny you should mention that because as of next season I was thinking of making it 25 per cent because I have done so well for you. You have done practically nothing to earn that money yet you want to take an even bigger slice of the cake. Well, bubbelah, you can forget it. And as I've come to see you at your request you can pay for the steak sandwich and the Diet Coke I've just had.' I walked out and didn't see him again for about two years.

I have to say that never again did he have the same success on or off the pitch, or even get close to it, so perhaps there is some justice after all.

Chapter Thirty-two

happily, there have been more good mates amongst my clients than bad ones. One of them is the wonderful Dennis Wise. I know he gets into the papers for all the wrong reasons sometimes, like being suspended or for having misunderstandings with taxi drivers, but he really is a super guy.

I don't want to go through all the ins and outs of that taxi incident – I'll let Dennis do that in his own book – but it was a fairly harrowing time for all of us. However, I do remember having a drink in a bar around the corner from the court when it was all over. There was a little Irish chap in there watching us knock back the champagne and we kept toasting each other with the word, 'lechayim'.

Eventually we asked him to join us. He had a glass of bubbly and when we did the toast he asked, 'I keep hearing you say that, what does it mean?'

I told him that it is a toast, like 'Cheers' in England, and that it means 'to life, for life, life, life'. I then asked what he was doing in the pub and he told me, 'I've been listening to his brother's trial. He got lechayim in court six.'

Another funny story connected with the case concerned a lovely lad who played at Wimbledon with Dennis called Vaughan Ryan. He and Dennis were monster friends even after Wisey left to join Chelsea and he turned up at the court every day and sat there all day when the case was on. Eventually, while we were outside the court waiting for the judge to give his verdict, Vaughan asked Dennis's lawyer, Gary Jacobs, 'What do you think will happen?'

Gary looked around and spotted the barristers from the other side standing close by.

'Well, I think Chelsea will have a very good season and Fulham could get promotion. And Terry Venables has built a good England squad and could do well in the European Championship.'

'No, I meant in the case,' said Vaughan.

'Well, I think Manchester United may find it tough in Europe but Arsenal may have an excellent season.'

Vaughan looked at him as if he was loopy. When Gary saw that the other barristers had moved off he explained, 'You should not have asked me about the case. I am not allowed to discuss it without my client's permission and although you are a very good friend of his I cannot tell you anything which is why I went on about Chelsea and Fulham and all that. Do you understand?'

'Yeah mate, of course I do, but a simple f*** off would have done.'

Another of my monster mates was Kenny Sansom. When Kenny was at Arsenal he had a bad leg injury which meant he had to spend some time in the Princess Grace hospital in London. I went to visit him one evening and found him sitting on his bed.

'Fancy a drink?' he asked.

'Yeah, I'll have a cup of tea or something.'

'No I mean a drink drink.'

'What do you mean?'

'Well, the doctor has told me I have to exercise my leg. So I thought we'd go down in the lift and I can walk up to the pub on the corner of the road and have a beer?'

'Are you sure, Ken?'

'Yes, check with the nurse if you like.'

So I did and she told me that was all right so out we went. As we got outside the hospital a cab went by and Kenny put his hand out and hailed it. 'Morton's please, Berkeley Square.'

'What are you doing,' I asked. 'I thought we were going to the pub.'

'No, no, Monster. Look it doesn't matter where we go but it's nicer in Morton's. When we get there I'll have a walk around the square for my exercise then we'll have that drink.'

Seven or eight hours later Kenny, who in a sense had been legless when we arrived, was now legless legless. It was about 2.30 am when we got back to the hospital and the big glass doors were locked. But we could see a porter inside so we started knocking on the door.

'Go away, or I'll call the police,' said the porter.

'No, you've got to let us in.'

'Go away, you'll disturb my patients.'

'But he is a patient.'

'No, go away.'

In the end I took Kenny back to my place and returned him to the hospital the following morning.

One of the questions I'm often asked is what is the main differenced between showbiz stars and football stars. I always answer by telling the story of seeing Pat Jennings, the goalkeeper, on *This Is Your Life*. When his father came from behind the curtain Pat shook his hand, emmes. He obviously loved his dad but he didn't give him a hug or a kiss, he shook hands. In showbiz everybody kisses everyone and that's how I grew up so I still do it. My players claim I'm a serial kisser, which is a nice line.

Another question I'm asked is if I've ever thought about being an agent for other sportsmen apart from footballers. I did once represent the boxer Lloyd Honeyghan and there's a funny story about him. After he won a British title or something he was looking for somewhere to celebrate with his friends so he tried to get into the famous club Tramp. It's a very exclusive place with a lovely lady at reception who has been there for years and seen everyone try all sorts of strokes to get in.

She said to Lloyd, 'Excuse me sir, are you a member?' He told her he wasn't.

'Are any of your friends members?' They weren't.

'In that case sir, I'm afraid you can't come in.'

'But I was here with Mickey Duff last week.'

'That's true, sir, but Mr Duff is a member so you came in with him but you can't come in without a member.'

'Do you know who I am?' said Honeyghan.

Quick as a flash she turned to the girl behind the desk and said, 'Quick, phone an ambulance, there's a man here who doesn't know who he is.'

Mention of the lovely Mickey Duff reminds me of the night he and that other boxing gentleman, Jarvis Astaire, arrived at Scribes while I was running the karaoke.

It so happened that Mickey had dyed his hair but it had clearly gone wrong because it had come out bright ginger. I couldn't resist being mischevious so I got Jarvis, who I knew had a very good voice, to sing a song. And when he'd finished I said, 'Now do one with your partner.'

'What partner?'

'Ginger Duff and Jarvis Astaire,' I said. Jarvis refused to talk to me for a long time after that but you've got to have a laugh haven't you?

Chapter Thirty-three

i 've never denied having a monster ego, but there are occasions when I feel entitled to be proud of something. One of those occasions was when I was invited to speak to the All-Party Committee for Culture, Media and Sport at the House of Commons. The Committee is a group of MPs who meet three or four times a year when a special guest gives a talk on a certain topic and then answers any questions the members want to ask.

The chairman, the Labour MP Joe Ashton, called to ask if I would be their guest. I was a bit suspicious at first because only a few weeks earlier another Labour MP, Kate Hoey, had mentioned my name in Parliament in connection with the football 'bungs' probe. I thought maybe they were trying to lead me into talking about the bungs issue but Joe Ashton assured me it was nothing to do with that and that they just wanted me to discuss the role of the agent in football.

As it turned out Kate Hoey was one of the few members of the Committee who wasn't present when I made my visit. I was told that as one of the Committee's members she had said that if they insisted on giving me the privilege of being their guest she would resign.

I don't know if she did but I was told that Joe Ashton said to her, 'Do what you like love, he's coming.'

I'm delighted I did go because I thoroughly enjoyed the experience of talking and answering questions in front of an audience of very famous faces. I didn't know all their names but I had seen every one of them on television many times. I also felt honoured because of the people who had previously been their guests: brilliant boxers like Muhammad Ali and Joe Frazier and footballers like the late, great Bobby Moore. Among those there were Tony Blair, the former Liberal leader David Steel and David Mellor, who once said of me: 'When you interview most people all you need is a sound bite, which is just a few words in reply to your question. But when you have Eric Hall on your show you get a banquet.'

Afterwards, Tom Pendry, who was then the Shadow Minister for Sport, took me into the bar for a drink and everyone in there came across to congratulate me. I had a nice surprise when I tried to buy them all a drink. Tom Pendry pointed to a sign on the bar which pointed out that because of an act passed in 1898-ish, only members of the House were allowed to buy drinks. And there was another sign that said that guests were not allowed to refuse any offer of a drink.

As a result by the time I left I really felt like an MP – Monster P**sed. But the drinking was not over because Tom Pendry then asked me what I was doing next. I told him that as I was feeling a bit worse for wear I thought I'd better go home to bed. He said that he was going to meet his friend Amie McDonald at the Rooftop Bar in the Hilton Hotel in Park Lane and insisted I went with him. And, being MP'd, I didn't have the strength to refuse.

When we arrived, another guest, who was there with a young lady, came over to talk to me. 'You're Eric Hall the agent,' he said. I wasn't MP'd enough not to know that he was right on that one but I had no idea who he was. 'My name is Owen Oyston, I'm the chairman of Blackpool,' he told me. I didn't realize that the next time I would see his name was when he was charged with rape and sent to prison.

After I had finished talking to him I bumped into John Fashanu, who I hadn't met since we fell out over that business with his brother Justin. But that incident was well behind us so we had a kiss and a cuddle and got a bit emotional. He told me he was waiting for Bruce Grobbelaar, the former Liverpool goalkeeper, to arrive. I left soon after so I don't know if Bruce arrived but it wasn't long after that meeting that I heard that John, Bruce and another goalkeeper, Hans Segers of Wimbledon, had been accused of 'bending' football matches and that they used to hold their meetings in a top London hotel.

I'm happy to say, however, that after two trials they were found not guilty. But that meeting in the Hilton was not the only connection I was to have with that trial. My other connection came from what I still consider to be one of the most monster coincidences in my life. It was to do with a Malaysian gentleman called Richard Lim who was also charged; he was alleged to have been the man who paid out the money.

On the day that the arrests were made I was at Birmingham City meeting their manager, the lovely Barry Fry, to discuss a few deals. When I returned to my home just off the Edgware Road in London it was dark but I could see that there was a group of people outside my front door. I immediately sensed that this was a press posse, and that was before I saw the unmistakable cameras used by the Fleet Street photographers. I had no idea what they wanted so I pushed my way through and put my key into the door. 'Excuse me,' shouted one of them, 'Are you, or do you know, Richard Lim?' I then turned around and another reporter shouted, 'Bloody hell, it's Eric Hall.' Suddenly there were cameras flashing and reporters yelling.

'Do you live here?' I was asked, so I told them that I did.

'Have you heard that John Fashanu, Bruce Grobbelaar and Hans Segers have been arrested?'

'Yes, I heard it on the car radio. What's it got to do with me?'

'Another man, Richard Lim, has also been arrested and his business address is this house.'

It then dawned on me that the flat upstairs from me was occupied by a Malaysian who I used to see regularly; we often ate at the same time – although never together – at a Spanish restaurant just around the corner. I couldn't believe it. Anyone putting two and two together could easily have come up with very short odds for putting me in the frame with them. I had been John Fashanu's agent, I was very friendly with both Bruce Grobbelaar and Hans Segers and I was living in the same house as the so-called 'bagman'.

There was also a lot of talk during the trial about 'the short man' – someone who had had meetings with the players and had many contacts in football. I'm not exactly tall and I don't think there are too many people in the game I don't know so that had tongues wagging about me as well. The final monster coincidence which emerged in the trial was that one of the code words used by the so-called conspirators when they phoned each other was 'Bubbelah', even though none of them was Jewish.

I swear, emmes, that I had nothing to do with any of the alleged events surrounding that trial, but there was so much circumstantial evidence that even I started to believe that I must have been involved somehow. I would not have been a bit surprised had the police wanted to interview me, but they never did.

Chapter Thirty-four

the events of the previous chapter lead me into even murkier waters concerning skulduggery and that almost unmentionable word, 'bungs'. The one story that really stands out in all my experience in the football business concerns a man called Eddie Ashby.

Ashby has over the years been closely connected with Terry Venables as an advisor in his personal and professional life. Loyalty to friends is one thing I most admire about Terry, but I am monster amazed that he allowed Ashby to have so much influence. I wouldn't take financial advice from a man who had forty-three failed businesses behind him and was declared bankrupt in 1991. This didn't stop Ashby though, and in 1997 he was sent to prison for a 'flagrant breach of the bankruptcy ban' for his involvement in the management of Spurs and Scribes West.

When I first met Ashby through Terry I could see no fault in him, but I was to discover that you trusted him at your peril when it comes to business deals. When Terry took over Portsmouth in 1996, someone from the club asked me if I could get them a deal with a kit manufacturer. I approached Colin Wooldridge, who had left Adidas and was now the promotions manager of Olympic Sport.

At first he wasn't too keen because they were chasing Premiership clubs but when I reminded him that Terry was involved and had been a winner at most places where he'd been in charge, he changed his mind and a meeting was set up between Colin, myself and Eddie Ashby. The meeting was to take place at my flat.

I threw figures at Colin that might not be big by Manchester United or Arsenal standards but Premiership clubs such as Coventry, Leicester, Southampton and Sheffield Wednesday would have been impressed, and by First Division standards, which is where Portsmouth were at the time, they were monster – a six-figure fee for using the kit plus all the extra training gear the players needed. It was almost three times the amount Portsmouth were receiving from the deal they had at the time with another kit manufacturer.

Colin agreed to what I knew was a marvellous deal for the club. I had already agreed a fee from Olympic for recommending them to the club (10 per cent of the total deal), and I felt I was also due a fee from Portsmouth for all the work I'd put in on their behalf. Normally I would have asked for 20 per cent but as I was already getting the Olympic fee I asked for the 10 per cent and had agreed this with Eddie Ashby even before we met Colin Wooldridge.

When Colin left Ashby and I discussed the deal which even he agreed was fantastic.

As he was leaving Ashby said, 'You're getting £40,000 out of all this, Eric, if it goes through?'

I agreed that was the figure and he said, 'So you want us to do the deal?'

'It's up to you. If you're not happy I'll try Adidas or some other company.'

'No, we're delighted with the deal, but I want £20,000 from you.'

'Pardon? In that case I want half the money I'm earning for you.'

'No, you are taking your commission already.'

'No I'm not. You're giving it to me with one hand and taking it back with the other.'

'I'm not talking about you paying it back to the club, I'm talking about you paying Eddie Ashby personally £20,000.'

'You what?' I screamed. 'You can f**k off now, get out of my flat.'

'Come on Eric, we can negotiate. Make it £15,000, it still leaves £25,000 profit for you.'

'You're not getting fifteen pence. I'm not paying you a bung.'

I threw him out and the deal with Olympic never went through.

Chapter
Thirty-five

bungs, bungs, bungs, bungs! That's all we've heard about in football over recent years and I have to say that in my humble-ish opinion it's all a load of nonsense. I threw Ashby out for asking for one, and he is the only person who has asked me for a bung. I have received and given what I consider to be presents after a deal has been successfully concluded to everyone's satisfaction, but never a bung. These presents weren't what I call 'please-do' gifts or incentives to sign or sell a player. They were received or sent after the act and I see absolutely nothing illegal or immoral about that.

I come from a showbiz world where this is the norm. I remember promoting a band called Geordie, who were managed by two Israeli boys called Ellis Elias and Eliot Cohen. After the band's song became a monster hit the managers sent me on a holiday to Tel Aviv, staying at the Hilton with full board and everything else paid for. I actually hated the holiday, not because I didn't like the place but because I was hanging around doing nothing for so long. I'd rather have taken the money it cost them and carried on working.

In those day the term used to describe the bungs paid to DJs in order to get them to play records on their shows was payola, but this was not the same thing. I'd got Geordie a huge hit because I had worked my cobblers off and their managers were grateful and gave me a present. Their next record was a flop so I got nothing.

It's the same in football and if there ever has been any so-called 'illegal' money paid to me by clubs I have always declared it to the Inland Revenue and VAT people. But because of the stupid rules laid down by the FA, the Football League or whoever, I can't invoice it as 'cash received for doing so-and-so transfer'; I have to use the lesson taught me by Robert Chase and say it's for some other service rendered.

In fact, when I've finished the deal for the player I now say, 'Mr Chairman, we'll now talk about my fee.' Instead of the player paying me for my services the clubs do it, which is why my clients always get the best of both worlds. They not only have the best agent in the business negotiating their contract, they get it for nothing. I have done that sort of deal with every major club in the country and I still say there is nothing wrong with it, just as I am prepared to state I could never see anything wrong with what George Graham did when he was manager of Arsenal.

When people say to me, 'George admitted taking bungs', I say what he admitted to was accepting a gift. I know George so well I'd be prepared to bet my life that there was no way in a million years that he would sign a player he did not want. If he did buy players he didn't think were any good and would not have bought unless he was given a bung I'd be the first to condemn him, just as in the old days I'd have condemned a DJ who plugged a record he hated because he was getting a few quid.

But it wasn't a case of the agent involved, Rune Hauge, saying, 'Take that, George, and buy my players.' The players had been signed and were doing the business on the pitch. Hauge had made a lot of money from the transfers and so he gave George a gift.

If anyone thinks I'm just defending an old friend with no proof let me tell you about another player, a Danish goalkeeper, who Hauge tried to sell to Arsenal. George told him, 'I don't need a goalkeeper, I've got David Seaman and I'm perfectly happy with the cover I've got for him. But I know that Alex Ferguson at Manchester United is looking for a keeper. Try him, tell him you know me.'

Hauge rang Ferguson who looked at the keeper and bought him. It was Peter Schmeichel and any United fan will tell you that it's probably the best signing he's made. They can thank George Graham for that but if George was buying players just for the bungs he would have taken Schmeichel. I tell you, bubbelahs, in my opinion, whatever George Graham was given it wasn't enough.

Chapter Thirty-six

*t*he ban imposed on me by Tottenham chairman Alan Sugar has been the cause of much comment and speculation since it happened and it's time I set the record straight.

When I first became an agent, for the Tottenham captain at the time, Steve Perryman, I wasn't necessarily a Spurs fan but I always enjoyed going there and dealing with the chairman, Irving Scholar. Naturally, I was delighted when my monster pal Terry Venables became manager. Then Terry, together with Alan Sugar, took over the club.

Not many people know this but Sugar is a relative of mine, not a blood relative but what we call a mishpocheh, which means family. My first cousin Melvyn Lewis is married to Ann and she is a first cousin to Alan Sugar. When Melvyn's daughter got married I sat at the same table as Alan Sugar and his mum and dad. Little did we know then the troubles that lay ahead between us, or that I would later say that his number plate, AMS 1, didn't refer to his initials but stood for A Monster Schmuck.

The problems I have had with Spurs started, of course, with the falling out of Terry Venables and Alan Sugar. Every night at Scribes

I'd hear Terry and Eddie Ashby talking about what a villain Sugar was, and he was this and that so it wasn't surprising that when Terry was sacked by Sugar he took him to court for unfair dismissal. Eventually Terry lost the case and the appeal was thrown out.

During the trial there had been a lot of fans outside the court who were shouting and screaming at Alan and his family, and even spitting at them and calling them things like 'Lousy Jews'. I was told only recently that one of the reasons Alan Sugar hated me was because he believed that I had paid for those people to go to the court and act as they did. But there is no way I would do that to any human being, no matter what their religion or how ever much we were in dispute.

I will own up to being involved in another pro-Venebles demonstration, however – one involving the wives of some of the Spurs players outside Sugar's home. But there was nothing violent or nasty about that – it was just the wives expressing their opinions. I can reveal now it was Neil Ruddock's wife, Sarah, and Paul Allen's wife, Monique, who organized that one, with a little help from yours truly.

Anyway, on the day Terry lost the case we left the court and Terry, Eddie Ashby and Terry's barrister Jonathan Crystal went to Scribes to drown their sorrows while I went to my office to do a bit of business. When I arrived there was a message on my fax machine from Tottenham Hotspur Football Club. It read,

'Dear Mr Hall,

This is to inform you that you are no longer welcome at Tottenham. You are barred for life.

This applies to both the ground and the training ground and while we cannot tell you who you can or cannot be an agent for it would be appreciated if you would no longer act for any of our players.'

It was signed by the club secretary Peter Barnes, who had been a monster friend of mine and it had been sent within forty minutes of the end of the court case. I'd have thought that Alan Sugar had better things to do at that time but he still found time to dictate that fax. So he obviously didn't like me but I have to say now that, with hindsight, perhaps I was wrong about him.

I've also since had cause to change my opinion of him because when I was monster ill, which I will deal with in the next chapter, my lovely mum Eva received a call from Alan Sugar asking how I was. He then told her, 'Whatever rows we've had in the past he's a good Yiddish boy and I don't want to see any harm come to him. And if you need anything please let me know, call me any time night or day.'

My mother was very touched by that and, when she told me about it, so was I. It takes a real man to do that and it makes me think that if I had to deal with Eddie Ashby, knowing what I know now, I'd have done exactly the same as Sugar did.

But Sugar's actions have cost me dearly because I lost David Howells and Vinny Samways, players with whom I could have done good transfer business, and also Justin Edinburgh, who was still there but was banned from using me as his contract negotiator. One player who stuck by me, however, was Neil Ruddock. He demanded a transfer and made sure I dealt with it. But there was a problem when John Scales, one of my clients, was available for transfer from Liverpool and I did a deal for him to join Leeds. Before we could complete the move, Scales received a call from Spurs saying they wanted him. It was made clear to him that there was no way Sugar would talk to me and in the end he negotiated his own deal with Tottenham and we fell out over it. So it did cost me but, as I say, it might have all been avoided if I had known at the time what I know now, and perhaps Alan Sugar might think the same.

There are a couple of other incidents on this subject which stick in my memory and actually make me chuckle to myself now and again. The first concerned the transfer to Tottenham of Jurgen Klinsmann, the first time around. A press conference to introduce Jurgen was televised live on Sky. During the conference Klinsmann was asked if there was anything special he wanted to do now he was based in London. He replied, 'When I have been here in the past with the German team all I have seen is the hotel and Wembley Stadium so now that I am living here I would like to see all the famous sights.' Alan Sugar cut in and said, 'In that case, Jurgen, you'll have to see Eric Hall, he's a right sight.'

Obviously he thought he was making a joke at my expense but what he really did was to make my day because that conference was being shown live all over Europe and having a name check was a monster boost for my ego.

On another occasion, when the club had a dinner for David Howells' testimonial, Sugar was called upon to make a speech. Despite my close relationship with David over the years I was not allowed to attend but I am told that Sugar said, 'I don't like making speeches but I'll do a few impressions instead. Who's this? Monster, monster, ish-ish, boom, boom, boom, he's a schmuck, are you mad?'

He spent five minutes doing an impression of me which I'm sure pleased everyone else at the dinner. I don't think he's ready to take over from Rory Bremner but again I feel honoured that he should take up so much of his time thinking about me. I think you like me really, Alan, and even if you don't, thanks again for that lovely conversation with my mum.

Chapter Thirty-seven

t he illness that resulted in Alan Sugar and, I was staggered to discover, thousands of others calling to express their concern about me, struck on 8 December 1997.

The nightmare started when I went, if you'll excuse the expression, to have a wee-wee at about 7 am. I saw to my horror that there was blood in my urine. Anyone who knows me is aware that I'm a monster hypochondriac (I'm the sort of person who will have on his headstone 'I told you I was ill, now do you believe me?'), so you can imagine how I felt looking at my own blood floating about in front of me. I wasn't in any pain but just the sight of the blood made me feel shaky so I immediately phoned my physician, Doctor Sawyer.

Of course, it was still too early in the morning to get hold of him, but when Tony, my assistant, arrived I tried again and the doctor told me to go and see him at his surgery in Wimpole Street immediately. Doctor Sawyer knows that I'm a hypochondriac but there was no hesitation on his part on this occasion.

When I went to see him he told me not to worry, although he was aware that I would anyhow, and said he would arrange for me to have tests later that day.

It so happened I was doing a TV show that day, and I do love a TV appearance, as my friends know only too well. I was taking part in a game show called *All Over The Shop* which was hosted by Paul Ross. Incidentally, the actress Nerys Hughes was also on the panel that day.

I told the doctor about the show, which was being filmed at lunchtime, and he told me to call him as soon as I'd finished. I left him and walked down the steps to the car where Tony was waiting. I can remember telling him what the doctor had told me and, I swear, bubbelahs, that was the last thing I remember until I woke up in hospital about six weeks later.

I did the TV show, made the call to the doctor and went for the hospital tests but although I did all that and was apparently normal to the people around me, it seems my brain had already cut out. I have no recollection of anything that happened to me after leaving the doctor.

To discover what was happening to me between seeing the doctor and waking up in University College Hospital in the middle of January, I have had to rely on the diary kept by my lovely sister Caroline and the memories of my lovely mum and all my other monster marvellous relatives and friends who visited, phoned and prayed for me during those dark days.

It seems that after receiving the tests I deteriorated rapidly so I was immediately taken into intensive care and given a blood transfusion. The first thing Caroline did when she heard of my condition was to cancel the holiday she and her family were due to start in Lanzarote the following day. She told me she'd spoken to the doctor and asked if she should go or not. He replied, 'Are you asking me if I think Eric is going to die?' When she said that she was he answered, 'I can't promise you that he won't.' That was enough for Caroline. The holiday was off and the calls started to the relatives all over the world. My brother Benny arrived, then my other brother Allen flew in from Spain and soon, I'm told, there was more of the Hall family in the hospital than there were patients.

The doctors still didn't know what was wrong with me and they wanted to take tests for everything including AIDS, but they couldn't do so without consent. I couldn't give it because by now I was in a coma, and my mum wouldn't because she was so upset. Eventually Caroline signed the consent form. Then she and my brothers sat up all night waiting for the results, all of which came up negative. So the doctors had to start looking for another explanation. But in the meantime my condition was deteriorating.

The next trauma for my family was on Sunday 14 December when Caroline and my two brothers came to visit and discovered that my face had gone lop-sided and that I was moaning like an animal. They thought I was having a fit. The nurse who was with me didn't seem to know what to do so they rushed out to get a doctor and he sent for a heart machine and a brain specialist. It transpired that I'd had a stroke.

Caroline was told that they did not expect me to make it through the night and so she started hitting the phone again. Uncles, aunts, cousins, second and third cousins, nephews and nieces again descended on the hospital.

The media were also driving everyone mad as they tried to find out what was happening to me. I've always got on well with journalists and realize they have a job to do but for Caroline especially it was a bad time. On one occasion she was told an uncle of mine was on the phone so she took the call only to be asked, 'Is that Eric Hall's sister?' She told them she was and the caller then said, 'This is such-and-such newspaper. Is Eric dead yet?' She was so upset that the hospital worked out a code system for her. Anyone calling for information about me had to use the name William before they could be put through.

By now my condition was so bad that mummy, Caroline and my brothers were losing patience. They still didn't know what was wrong with me but were told that it could be the blood infection *e-coli* or septicaemia but they didn't know why it was affecting me in the way it was.

Finally Caroline cracked and demanded they find the best blood specialist in the world, whether he came from Timbuktu or China. It turned out that he was less than a mile away, at the University College Hospital, and his name was Professor Machin. He looked at my blood and needed only minutes to come up with the answer to the problem that had baffled everone else. I had TTP – otherwise known as Thrombotic Thrombocytopenic Purpura. If I had been awake at the time I would probably have said, 'That's easy for you to say, bubbelah, but what the hell does it mean?'

The illness was something to do with the level of my platelets, the microscopic things in your blood which stop it clotting. The normal level is 200-ish but I was down to single figures and at one time as low as two which is about as close to death as you can get.

Chapter Thirty-eight

the diagnosis was not the end of the problem but, looking back on it now, it was probably the beginning of the end because finally everyone knew what they were up against and we had the top man in the world on our side.

The blood disease I had contracted attacks only one in a million people but I had an aggravated version which took the odds to probably one in three million. If I'd been aware of this at the time my ego would no doubt have been impressed by those sort of odds. Instead I was still in a coma and getting worse.

Professor Machin wanted me to move me to his hospital but before he could do so my condition deteriorated even more so I was taken to the National Hospital for Neurology instead. It was from there that Caroline received a call saying that my kidneys, lungs and liver had all failed and that I was on dialysis and a life-support machine. This started a row amongst my family as they were all trying to donate various organs but couldn't decide who should give me what. In the meantime Professor Machin wanted to start treating the TTP but couldn't do so while I was in this condition because the only machine available for that treatment was at University College Hospital.

I was eventually moved to UCH and although I was still in a coma the platelet count was rising as a result of the treatment. By Christmas Eve it was up to almost 200 which was very good. Then, as the Intensive Care Unit was to be closed for the holiday, I was moved again, this time to the Rosenheim Wing of the hospital across the road.

At 7 am on Christmas morning my family was told that although the platelet level had dropped slightly the doctors were happy with my progress. I even opened my eyes, so I'm told, but I didn't know what was going on. They all went home to have their Christmas lunch and Caroline and her family were just about to sit down to their meal when the telephone rang. She was told that the platelet count was down to seven, that I was probably dying and that she should get to the hospital as soon as possible. She should also inform the rest of the family about the situation.

Christmas dinner, like the holiday, was forgotten and they all returned to the hospital, only to discover that I was about to be moved again. I needed intensive care and, as the unit was closed, I had to be switched to the Middlesex Hospital. I wish I'd been the agent for all these moves I was making because I could have earned a fortune.

For the next two weeks my platelet level readings look like the Alps – it was all ups and downs. My lovely family would be happy and then the reading would drop suddenly and they would go into another depression.

There were also times when, would you believe, I became violent. On one occasion when that I had more tubes in me than London Transport own I pulled one of them out of my throat. This was a mistake as I ruptured my vocal cords and was left sounding like a Jewish Louis Armstrong. I also tried to strangle and kick a couple of nurses and slapped my sister across the face.

By 7 January Professor Machin had decided that he wanted to give me an experimental drug called Difibrolite, which had been tried on only fifty patients worldwide. Again my closest relatives – they still hadn't decided who was officially my next of kin – were asked to give permission. After being told that so far no side-effects had emerged they agreed.

For three days it was still up and down and then, on 11 January 1998, I woke up and for the first time since arriving in the hospital on 8 December I looked around the room. I then complained that my mouth was dry and demanded an ice lolly.

That should have been the end of the nightmare for myself and my family but, as that Irish comedian Jimmy Cricket used to say, there's more, there's more. I was moved to the Wellington Hospital – another transfer deal I could have handled – to convalesce. I did a deal with the hospital whereby if they let me out for a few hours to do such-and-such an interview or make the odd personal appearance at a club or whatever I would get back on time and not overdo it.

In February I was finally allowed to go home, on the condition that I had someone with me all the time and that I attended out-patients regularly for blood transfusions. Everything was fine for a month and then my platelet readings suddenly dropped dramatically and I was sent back to intensive care. I was there for five weeks and the inactivity was driving me potty. I was desperate to get back to work and see all my players and do my Saturday night LBC radio show. I had arranged a long time before for my old friend Frankie Vaughan to be the guest on the Easter weekend and so I decided that I would definitely leave hospital in time to do that particular show. Caroline and the hospital staff were against it but I told them that I was leaving, with the drip still in my arm if necessary, and so, on Good Friday, I was allowed to go home, with the same conditions as before. On Saturday morning I was sorting out which of Frankie's records I was going to play that night when the lights went out again. My brother Benny arrived to spend the day with me and found me lying on the floor, back in a coma.

This time the TTP (I won't spell it out in full again) had affected my lungs – they were now full of small clots of blood – so I had to spend another five weeks in hospital. Eventually the clots disappeared, the platelet levels were high and stable and I returned home. I'm glad to say everything is still fine. But the good Professor Machin has told me the TTP will never disappear. They still don't know what caused it; it could be a bacteria that has been lurking about inside me for fifteen years or it could be a virus I picked up just days before I was struck down. The good news is that having survived the initial attack it is now what they call a controllable disease. As long as I am closely monitored there is no reason they cannot catch a relapse in time and solve the problem with a blood transfusion so, God willing, you are all going to have to put up with me for a long time yet.

Chapter Thirty-nine

While my family had to put up with all the ups and downs of the dark days I, of course, knew nothing about it so had the best of the deal really. However, there were some bad moments which I still remember vividly, even though they didn't seem to be real at the time. I think they may explain the attacks I made on the nurses.

I had nightmares that were so real that I can still see them happening when I think about it six months later. On one occasion I thought that three nurses had come into my room, tied me up and put a gag around my mouth – something a lot of people would like to have done and still do. Then they took me on a red London bus to Woodford in Essex, which just happens to be where my mum Eva lives. Then they took me into a house and tried to rape me. I should be so lucky you might say, but unlike the lovely nurses who were looking after me most of the time, these were the ugliest nurses you've ever seen. I was fighting and screaming and I finally escaped by crawling through one of those cat-flaps in the door before getting another red bus which took me home.

Due to the health plan I had, and I had paid monster contributions into it for many years, I was entitled to a twenty-four-hour nursing service. So a few weeks after I came out of the coma I was sitting in my room watching a film called *Mr Skeffington*, which starred Bette Davis and Claude Rains, when the nurse who was taking over the 3 pm to 10 pm shift walked in.

It turned out to be a very camp male nurse who made Larry Grayson look like an all-in wrestler. 'Hello Monster, Monster, lovely to see you, how are we today, is there anything you want?' he said.

'Hello bubbelah. Yes, I'm a bit thirsty... any chance of a glass of water?'

I dozed off before he came back and when I woke up again he was sitting in the armchair facing the television shouting, 'Go on you beauty, go on you beauty.' He was watching the horse racing on Channel Four.

I thought I'd gone into a coma again and had been out for three days or something because one minute I was watching a lovely film and the next there were all these horses on the screen.

'What's happening?' I asked.

'Oh, there's your water, Monster, you'll enjoy that.'

'Have I been asleep long?' I asked.

'No, only a couple of minutes.'

'What's happened to the film then?'

'I turned it over because I want to watch the racing.'

'Are you sure?'

'Yes, I like racing and my friend gave me a tip. It's running in the next race.'

'Excuse me, I was enjoying that film. Can you put it back on again?'

'Oh, come on, let me watch the racing. I always watch it on a Saturday.'

I was very aggressive at that time, because of the treatment I was getting, so I yelled, 'Put the f**king film back on,' and I don't think I was wrong. Who was paying the bills, him or me?

On another occasion, and I want to point out that they were rare occasions, I had a nurse who was doing the late shift, from 10 pm until about 7 am. Now I don't mind admitting that all my life I've slept with the light on – maybe I've always been nervous but that's the way it is. So I had my bedside lamp on as I listened to Douglas Cameron, who was doing my LBC show for me, before I again dozed off. When I woke up there was total silence and absolute blackness. I thought I'd either gone blind or I was dead and I panicked. Bear in mind I was still not 100 per cent well in my head, but then I never really was, and I must have started shouting and hollering.

'What's the matter there, man?' I heard someone say, and suddenly the light went on and there was the nurse.

'Don't ever do that again,' I shouted, a bit more aggressively than I should have, but I was monster terrified.

'I'm sorry but you were asleep so I turned the light and radio off.'

'Well, turn it back on again.'

Finally I calmed down and asked her to get me a drink. She did so and then she came and sat by the bed and said what I thought was 'You due.'

'Due what, a tablet or something?'

'No, you Jewish,' she said.

'Yes, I am bubbelah, why?'

'You won't go to heaven unless you believe in Jehovah,' she said.

Suddenly I realized that I was being lectured by a Jehovah's Witness. If I was at home I could have just closed the front door but not only was I trapped in a hospital room I was also having transfusions every couple of hours. And here was a nurse telling me that I wouldn't go to heaven and that having blood transfusions is wrong.

Again I did my nut, but yet again I think I was entitled. They were some of the bad moments I had which I could later forget, but there were also sad moments which I will always remember.

When I came out of the coma I had muscle wastage in my legs and needed to get plenty of exercise so I began taking walks along the hospital corridors. There were all sorts of patients there for all sorts of illnesses and one day I was going along the corridor when a young boy, with his mother holding his hand, came towards me.

He couldn't have been more than eight or nine and he'd had all his hair shaved off. We passed each other a few times and he kept looking at me and finally as we crossed again he said, 'I told you, Mummy, look, it's Monster, Monster.'

At the time, being an egomaniac, I was delighted and later I asked my nurse about the lad. 'Yes, he's always talking about you, he's a big Tottenham fan,' she said. I asked what he was in hospital for, thinking it was some sort of children's illness. 'He's got cancer,' she replied. I was devastated and what made it worse was that I never saw him again and, to be honest, I was too frightened to ask what had happened to him. But it had a monster effect on my thinking. I've been asked if what happened to me changed my way of life but I have to say that what it did really was to rubber stamp my life. I've always been one of those guys who if I earn £1 I'll spend no more than ninety-nine pence. Now, having seen that little lad and many others in the hospital and having survived, God willing, if I earn £1 I spend £1. Before my attitude to life was let's go for it, now it's let's monster, monster go for it.

While I was on my walks in the hospital I went by the room of another patient, a big man wearing a dressing gown who was sitting on the end of his bed as I passed by. He smiled so I smiled back but I carried on walking. 'Don't give us the bum's rush,' he called.

'Pardon?'

'Don't just smile at me, stop for a chat,' he said. 'You know who I am.'

'Sorry bubbelah, I'd love to chat to you but I don't know you.'

'I work for your favourite football team,' he said.

I couldn't place him until he laughed and said, 'It's Tottenham, my name is Claude Littner and I'm the chief executive of the club.'

He was in there having chemotherapy and every day after that we had a chat. It seems everywhere I go I can't get away from that bloody Tottenham.

One day when we met he was with two ladies who he introduced as his wife and his mother. 'Do me a favour, Eric,' he said. 'My mother loves your radio show so will you say bubbelah and emmes and ish for her? So I did and she loved it and finally I said monster, monster and she went into hysterics. I'm glad to say that Claude is well and still chief executive at Spurs.

One of the amazing things that happened soon after I came out of the coma was that one of my clients, Tim Sherwood who was then captain of Blackburn, called.

'How are you, Monster?'

'Yes, I'm fine,' I answered, even though I was still out of it really.

'Good, because I need your help. I'm negotiating a new contract and I'm with the chief executive John Williams. Can you talk to him?'

I agreed and Williams said, 'I'll come to London if you want me to Eric.'

'No we'll do it now. How much are you offering?'

He laughed but didn't answer. 'What have you raised the money to?' I asked again.

He said something I didn't hear so I kept saying 'How much?'. Finally I said, 'It's not enough,' and I heard him say to his chairman, 'See, I told you. He said it's not enough and we haven't even mentioned money yet.' Then he said to me, 'We thought you might have mellowed with your illness but you're the same as ever, Monster.' Bless him, he had a good laugh.

Another client who came to see me nearly every day was Dennis Wise who came with his girlfriend Claire. I call him a client but he's really a monster mate like all my players. When they visited for the first time I was lying there full of all these tubes and was hardly able to talk. Dennis suddenly burst into tears, and would you believe it, Claire passed out. So I pressed my emergency button and the nurse rushed in. She came to me and asked what was wrong and I tried to tell her about Claire by pointing to the corner of the room. Finally she saw Claire and went to attend to her. Funnily enough, after I'd left hospital Dennis and Claire were invited to the premiere of Vinny Jones's movie, *Lock, Stock and Two Smoking Barrels*. I saw him a few days later and asked him how they enjoyed it. 'We had to leave, Claire passed out again,' he said. I hope Vinny didn't look as bad as I did.

Two other regular visitors were Terry Venables and Terry Fenwick. They came just after the time I'd pulled the tube out of my mouth and damaged my vocal cords.

'How are you?' said Terry.

'OK. The only problem is that I might never be able to talk the way I used to,' I said.

And I heard him lean over to Terry Fenwick and say, 'May be a problem for him but it'll be a Godsend to us.' You were joking, weren't you Tel?

Chapter Forty

how can I possibly express my gratitude, amazement and for a change, the sheer monster humility I felt and still feel over the reaction to my illness? I still find it difficult to believe that I received over 7,000 written messages from all over the world and that the phones at the hospital and at my sister's home never stopped ringing. There are sacks of cards that I am now reading for the first time and I want to thank everyone who took the time and trouble to write.

They came from people in all walks of life, from the stars I've met to the lovely people who have seen me on television, listened to my radio shows or read my newspaper column. It would be silly of me to try and mention particular names, but if I was lined up against the wall and told I'd be shot if I didn't pick out one special person then I'd quickly give in, like the coward I am, and say it's got to be Bob Hope.

When I was a kid going to the Saturday morning pictures I loved all those road movies with Bob Hope and Bing Crosby. He's been one of my favourite comedians and people ever since. So when I saw the telegram from Bob and Dolores Hope wishing me a speedy recovery I almost died – again.

I had the monster pleasure of speaking to Bob when I was doing my LBC radio show in which I phone famous stars (mainly singers), who then also talk to the listeners. My guest was not Bob but his lovely wife Dolores, who was once a very good nightclub singer. In fact, she told me that she was singing in a New York club when she met Bob. His friend and fellow actor George Murphy told Bob what a great singer Dolores was and how beautiful she was and to go and see her in cabaret. Bob wasn't too bothered and really had to have his arm twisted. But he soon realized that George was right and when he heard Dolores sing that lovely song 'I Only Have Eyes For You' he knew that in future he would only have eyes for her. They married and have been together for over seventy years, which is totally incredible as far as I'm concerned.

I invited Dolores on to my show because in 1997 she had made a new album and, despite her age, (I didn't break the golden rule and ask how old she was but you can figure it from the time she's been married) she still had a lovely voice. I played some tracks from the album and she chatted to the listeners who called in. Then, as I was playing the last number and saying goodbye to her off air, I asked, 'How is Bob? I'm told he's not been too well.' She told me there had been a story in an American newspaper a week or so earlier stating that he had actually died. When he read the story over breakfast Bob said to her, 'For a dead man I have one hell of an appetite.'

Dolores then told me he was feeling much better and then she said, 'In fact Eric, he's listening on the other extension. Would you like a word?' Was she sure! I couldn't believe my luck. One of the world's great superstars was talking to East End Eric.

I asked how he was doing and we had a little chat and then, being as monster cheeky as ever, I asked him, 'Tell me Bob, you and Dolores have been married over seventy years but do you still like a little bit of hanky panky?'

He replied, 'Well, Eric, we have adjoining bedrooms now but if Dolores fancies a kiss and a cuddle she starts whistling our song, 'I Only Have Eyes For You', and I knock on the door and go into her room.'

'And what if you fancy a kiss and a cuddle?' I asked.

'I knock on her door and ask, "Dolores, did I hear you whistling?".'
He may be nearing his century but his sense of humour is as sharp as ever.

This story reminds me of the marvellous Bing Crosby, Bob's road movie partner. On the day he died the news came through while Nicky Campbell was doing his BBC radio show. Nicky decided to play one of Bing's records as a tribute and picked out the great Irving Berlin number 'Cheek To Cheek'. Unfortunately he'd forgotten the first line of the song is 'Heaven, I'm in Heaven'.

My radio show has brought me so much pleasure, as have most of the things I've done in my life. It's given me the opportunity to speak to many of my idols, apart from Bob Hope. Do I love to name drop? Well, here are just some of the stars I've had on my show: Frankie Laine, Eddie Fisher, Guy Mitchell, Andy Williams, Rosemary Clooney, Al Martino, Connie Francis, Neil Sedaka, Engelbert Humperdinck, Max Bygraves, Kay Starr, Sacha Distel, Howard Keel, Frankie Vaughan, Donald O'Connor, Buddy Greco, The Mills Brothers, Jimmy Roselli, Luke Goss of Bros (for the younger listeners), Russ Conway, Norman Wisdom, Frank Ifield, Edmund Hockridge and many more.

One of the stars who hosted the show during my absence was the lovely Frankie Vaughan. The first time he should have been on as a guest was when I was found by my brother Benny after I'd been taken ill. The producer of the show had arranged for Johnny Speight to stand in for me but had forgotten to tell Frankie that I would not be there.

Frank turned up at the studio and told the receptionist why he was there and the producer suddenly realized he had a problem.

But, thinking on his feet, he explained to Frank what had happened and said, 'Instead of being Eric's guest, how would you like to stand in for him instead?' The producer was able to stop Johnny Speight in time and Frank spent three hours talking to the hundreds of listeners who phoned in, and played some of his own records, as well as many of my favourites which I'd already lined up for the show. When I had recovered Frank came to see me and said, 'Eric, that was one of the best nights I've had in show business for a very long time.'

I know what he means, because I love every Saturday night as well. I love talking to my listeners, many of them ladies, who are, shall I say, mature enough to remember the kind of music I love.

Frankie Laine typifies that middle-of-the-road music and I've had him on my show twice. He's eighty-five now but his voice is as good as ever-ish but I was a bit worried about his hearing the first time he appeared. One of my listeners told him her granddaughter had been named after one of his most popular songs. 'Which one do you think it is?' she asked. Frankie thought for a moment then said, 'Was it "Champion The Wonder Horse"?'

'No, it was "Georgia",' snapped the listener before slamming down the phone.

On his second visit I got a call from someone named Terry in Knightsbridge. He was put through and I said, 'Hello, is that Terry?'

'Yep.'

'Do you want to talk to Frankie?'

'Yep.'

It took only two 'yeps' for me to recognize the voice of Terry Venables. Well, I had known him for over thirty years.

'Is that you, Tel?' I asked.

He then owned up and I asked Frankie Laine if he knew who Terry Venables was.

'Of course I do, he's your top football coach,' he replied, which monster amazed me. How did someone living in San Diego know who the England coach was? Terry then told him that one of his hits was his all-time favourite songs. It was 'A Woman In Love'. As Tel is a great singer I got my own back and said, 'Sing it for Frankie will you?'

He wasn't too sure about that, but finally gave in and started singing, 'Your eyes are the eyes of a woman in love' and then Frankie joined in. What a double act and what a monster thrill for myself and my monster, monster listeners.

Chapter Forty-one

One of the guests who appeared on my radio show was Dorothy Squires, that wonderful Welsh lady who used to sing beautiful ballads. She had been a guest before I was taken ill and when I was well enough to take calls she rang to ask how I was and to wish me well. What I didn't know, because I had been in a coma so long, was that Dorothy was also in hospital when she made that call and, in fact, died not long after making it. I felt so upset when I found out I just burst into tears. I just hope she realized I was unaware that she was so ill but it says so much about her that she took the time out to worry about my health.

It is things like that which make me feel so humble about my experience. So many people called with flowers, often travelling a long way, only to be told I was too ill to see anyone. My old friend Steve Harley was one of the first to arrive. He had a huge bunch of flowers and left them with a card which said, 'Get well soon, Monster, and make me smile.' 'Make Me Smile' was, of course, the title of the hit record I promoted for him and which got into the charts again quite recently after it was featured in *The Full Monty*. Steve told Caroline, 'When he's better again tell Eric that without him no-one would ever have heard of me.'

Max Bygraves visited with flowers, Russ Conway was a regular caller, my uncle Spencer called almost every day from America, baskets of fruit arrived from various TV shows I'd appeared in and the lovely, lovely Barbara Windsor took the phone call record. She called Caroline four times a day, every day. She called in the morning to see what sort of night I'd had, then at midday to see how my treatment had gone, then at 4 pm to check again and at 10 pm to tell Caroline to give me a goodnight kiss. Thanks for all the kisses, Barbara.

I'm delighted to say that I will soon be producing a record with her. My old friend Ray Levy of Telstar Records called me recently and mentioned Barbara. 'A great star and personality, it's a pity she doesn't sing because I'd love to do a record with her,' he said.

'Are you sure, bubbelah? Did you know that Barbara started in show business singing with the Ronnie Scott band? And I have to tell you that when I went to her birthday party last year she got on stage in front of an all-star audience, sang "You Made Me Love You" and there was not a dry eye in the house. It was something I'll never forget.'

So she's doing the record and it will take me right back to my days with EMI when I produced the Hylda Baker and Arthur Mullard hit.

And now the end is near, as Frank Sinatra sang. Not of me, I hope, but of this book. I've tried to be factual and tried to tell everything I remember of my life that I think will be interesting to, hopefully, a lot of readers.

I've also attempted to thank and mention all the people who have helped me during my life, both in showbiz and football. And most of all I hope I've been able to thank those who helped me to stay alive. I would like to put very high on that list Professor Sam Machin, Doctor Simon Cohen and all the nurses and staff of the University College Hospital who were so monster fantastic when my life was in the balance.

I know I was a bit rude and aggressive at times but honestly, bubbelahs, I wasn't myself and I want to apologize if I upset you and to tell you all that I love you.

I'm also indebted to my assistant Tony who, during my illness, so I'm told, got the sack more often than Santa Claus, and my speech therapist without whom I would not be working today.

I want to finish by thanking the best family in the world: lovely Caroline, Benny and Allen, my lovely nieces and nephews, uncles, aunts and cousins and mispoche. And most of all I want to thank my lovely mum Eva who never left my side through it all and who said that if I had died she would have as well. When I first left home my mum stood on the doorstep and cried, 'Don't go, bubbelah, when will I see you again, bubbelah, who will look after you, bubbelah?' I told her I was only moving from Stamford Hill to the Edgware Road, I'd be back for my dinner once I'd moved in and anyway, I was thirty-seven years old.

So that's it. I hope you've enjoyed it. I'm just happy I was around to finish it and, after what I've been through there's only one toast with which to finish:

Lechayim! To Life!

Index